THE 1938 TUBE STOCK

Piers Connor

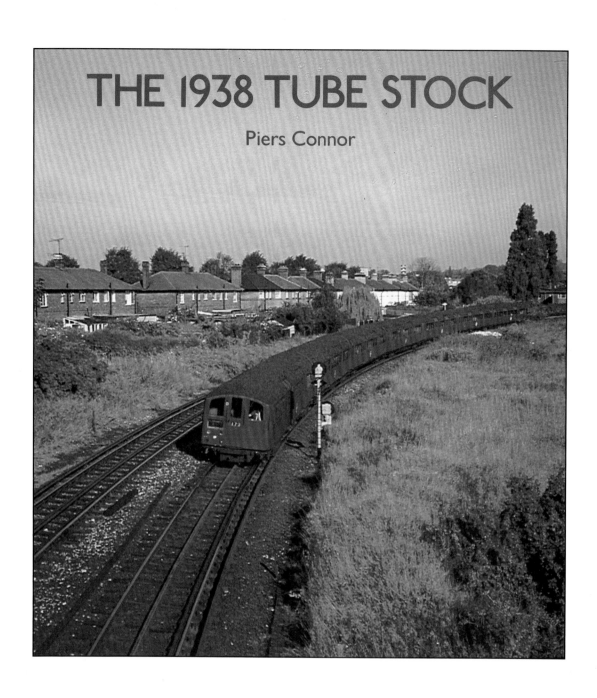

IN ASSOCIATION WITH

LONDON TRANSPORT
MUSEUM

Capital Transport

FOREWORD by J Graeme Bruce OBE, BSc(Eng), FIEE, FIMechE, FCIT

The 1938 Tube Stock spanned virtually half a century of service to the London public, operating mainly on the Northern, Bakerloo and Piccadilly Lines for a considerable part of this period. I am particularly pleased to provide this foreword to the story, which happens to cover a major part of my working life. I took part in the original testing of the 1935 Experimental Stock and the original deliveries of the 1938 Tube Stock. I was actively concerned with trouble-shooting during the period of teething troubles and subsequently had to look after the maintenance of the 1935 Experimental Stock based in Northfields Depot, where all the problems of the innovative features were all too obvious. After the outbreak of the war, I had to recommend their storage as they were absorbing too much skilled manpower in keeping them serviceable. After the end of the war, first as a member and then as Chairman of the Rolling Stock Programme Committee, I was concerned in initiating many of the complicated train reformations and transfers between lines which are described in some detail in the text.

The 1938 Tube Stock was a major advance in the design of trains for running in the restricted clearance tunnels of London. Graff Baker, the Chief Mechanical Engineer responsible for the design, encouraged innovative solutions to technical problems and in obtaining these solutions he took advantage of the frontiers of engineering knowledge available at the time such as welding techniques, the development of plastics and the advances in electric circuitry and switchgear. He subsequently, but not for the 1938 Tube Stock, encouraged the use of extruded aluminium, and of rubber in shear for suspension, developed for 1959 Tube Stock after his death.

With so much innovation, it was very exciting to be associated with the introduction and operation of the 1938 Tube Stock. There were troubles in plenty but most of them were eventually overcome, the most recalcitrant being the problems associated with the original rotary compressor, which was basically too delicate for the rough life on Underground service. However, at the time of its introduction it was the only machine which could be accommodated satisfactorily under the solebar of the tube car as then designed.

Various memories of the 1938 Tube Stock come to mind, such as crawling underneath a train in a tube tunnel to demonstrate the arrangement necessary to lock up the shoegear in an emergency; spending hours and hours tediously watching meters to try and locate stray currents which might open doors in the tunnel while the train was in motion, only to be rewarded at Clapham Common without seeing the meters move (on this occasion I was accused by my betters of not paying attention, or even looking for female distraction on the platform); being concerned with wiring alterations to ensure the safety of the door circuits but making a mistake with the special 9-car motor cars which almost cost me my job; testing the newly designed D-to-D coupler for connecting incompatible automatic couplers in an emergency; using a train of 14 cars with this contraption between two 7-car trains, one right way and one wrong way, and then being unable to get them apart at Edgware, thus causing a 30-minute delay in service.

These incidents directly affected me personally, but subsequently there were many others where my involvement was more remote. It is good that the ups and downs of the life of the 1938 Tube Stock have been recorded by the capable interpretation of Piers Connor.

ISBN 185414 115 5

Published by Capital Transport Publishing
38 Long Elmes, Harrow Weald, Middlesex

Printed by Winchmore Press,
Fowler Road, Hainault, Ilford, Essex

Photographs on pages 1 and 4 are by Brian Hardy, on page 3 by LT Museum and on page 5 by Chris Wilson.
The cover painting is by Ray Stenning.

AUTHOR'S NOTE

In the years of preparation of this book, I have received willing help from many people either directly or indirectly. In particular I must thank Gordon Hafter, from the time when he was Director of Mechanical Engineering of the London Underground, J. Graeme Bruce, formerly Chief Operating Manager, R.J. Greenaway, B.R. Hardy, F.W. Ivey and D.F. Croome. The present staff of London Underground Ltd have also helped, both directly and indirectly in the provision of material for this book. To them, and all those others who have contributed to this work over the years, my thanks.

Great Bookham, August 1989   PIERS CONNOR

Contents

Introduction

The story of the 1938 tube stock, by definition, covers the history of the 1,121 cars built as part of the expansion of the tube lines under the 1935-40 New Works Programme which were known as the 1938 tube stock. But it also covers several other similar types of car which became part of the 1938 fleet and some less similar cars which were converted for use in 1938 stock train formations. One type which became part of the 1938 stock was the experimental 1935 tube stock, 24 cars in all, which were built as prototypes of the 1938 stock and 18 of which were later converted to run as 1938-type trailer cars. The 'less similar' cars which are included in the 1938 tube stock story, are the '58 trailers'. These were 1927-built trailers taken from 'Standard' stock trains and converted to work in 1938 stock train formations. The title '58 trailers' was adopted so as to distinguish them from ordinary, unconverted 1927 trailers and from 1938 trailers. The number 58 actually referred to the number of cars

eventually converted, not, as was usual on the London Underground, to the date of the cars. The use of the date (usually the expected date of the first to enter service) to distinguish batches of cars was a custom begun before the First World War and which has continued ever since on the London tube lines. The 58-trailers name tag was a rare exception to this rule and, indeed, was initially only semi-official. Later, it became recognised throughout the system.

The other group to become part of the 1938 stock fleet was the 1949 tube stock. This stock could be included as one of the 'similar types' mentioned above. It consisted of 91 cars, built after the Second World War, which were needed to allow a reorganisation of the 1938 stock. The 1938 stock train formations had become disorganised because of the war and the new cars were introduced to allow new formations to be made up under what was known as the 1949 Uncoupling Programme. The 1949 date was used to

distinguish these cars not only because of their newer build but also because they had some equipment differences. One of these differences was the bogies and this led to their early demise. During the culling of the stock in the mid-1970s, the 1949 cars were all withdrawn in preference to 1938 cars because, although they were newer, they had non-standard bogies.

With the above variations in mind, the 1938 stock can be broken down into batches as follows:

Build date	Builder	DM Cars	NDM Cars	UNDM Cars	Trailer Cars	Total
1938	Metro-Cammell	644	107			751
1938	Birmingham		99		271	370
1927	Converted 1938				58	58
1949	Birmingham			70	21	91
1935	Converted 1949				+18	18
1938	Converted 1949		−22	+22		
	Final Totals	644	184	92	368	1288

The dates mentioned in this table are somewhat arbitrary. Although the 1938 stock began delivery in 1938, delivery was not actually completed until two years after the end of the war in 1945. The 1949 programme was also very slow in completion and was not finished until 1953.

Some of the types of car introduced into the 1938 fleet were new to the London tubes. In the table above, only driving motor cars and trailers were already recognised tube car types in 1938. The Non Driving Motor (NDM) – a trailer car body (i.e. no driving cab) but with traction motors and control gear – was a new type in 1938. Also, in 1949, the Uncoupling Non Driving Motor (UNDM) appeared. This was a Non Driving Motor with a set of driving controls fitted in a cabinet at one end. These controls were limited and only allowed shunting and uncoupling movements. The controls were housed in what was called a 'shunting control cabinet'.

Chapter 1
The LPTB's New Tube Stock

On 1st July 1933 the London Passenger Transport Board came into being. Formed to govern a unified public transport system for the Greater London area, it took over the large group of companies which had, until that time, run the bus, tram and Underground rail services in the nation's capital. Amongst the largest of these companies were the London General Omnibus Company, the London United Tramways, the Central, Bakerloo, Piccadilly and Hampstead tube lines, the City and South London Railway (the pioneer tube line which, with the Hampstead tube and its extensions, was known as the Morden-Edgware line), the District Railway and the Metropolitan Railway, which was the only company in the list not actually under the same ownership prior to the formation of the LPTB. All the other companies were part of the 'Underground Group', as the Underground Electric Railways of London Ltd was called.

The formation of the LPTB, soon known to the public as London Transport, provided a not unintentional opportunity to develop new routes, remove wasteful competition and expand existing services. Even before 1933, many schemes had been mooted for the extension of Underground services. 1923 saw a scheme to extend the Hampstead and Bakerloo lines northwards beyond Edgware and Watford to St Albans, and about the same time a southern extension of the Hampstead & City line to Sutton was proposed. It only got as far as Morden in 1926 after a deal was struck with the sitting tenant south of the river Thames, the Southern Railway. If the Underground would not try any more incursions into Southern territory, the deal went, the Southern would not oppose the Hampstead & City extension from Clapham to Morden.

Of course the only loser was the travelling public of Sutton which has been saddled ever since with a series of meandering routes wending their way through South London to the edges of the City and West End when they might have had direct routes to both areas by Underground. It was partly to prevent a continuation of such situations that the LPTB was created and, soon after its formation, a series of schemes to rationalise and expand Underground services was drawn up. The schemes were to be spread over a five-

year period and were collectively known as the 1935-40 New Works Programme. Both tube and surface lines were involved and the programme included a vast rolling stock renewal scheme in addition to new cars required for new extensions. It was the rolling stock part of the programme which concerns this story and, in particular, the new stock required for the tube lines, which was to become known as the 1938 Tube Stock.

The 1935-40 New Works Programme was divided into four main schemes. These were classified into four areas and became known as the Western, North Western, Northern and North Eastern extensions. Each of them involved an extension to an existing line, each involved at least one of the tube lines and each needed new rolling stock.

Not surprisingly, the Programme was expensive; it was to cost £40 million. Equally unsurprising was the need to get financial assistance from the government. This was forthcoming (in the shape of guaranteed loans) because of the desire to reduce unemployment, but it did produce a situation often seen in such cases, which has a bearing on this story. The situation concerned the proportional system of allocating money for new trains which, as will become apparent as this story continues, made for a curious policy during the early years of the programme and which ultimately caused lots of juggling with numbers to get what was actually needed to provide a viable service on all the lines concerned.

Each of the New Works schemes was ambitious. The Western scheme involved a new branch for the Central Line to Denham from a junction at North Acton with the existing route to Ealing Broadway. The line was to run parallel with the existing Great Western Railway line. The North Western scheme involved a new branch of the Bakerloo running from Baker Street, parallel to the existing Metropolitan line but under it, to Finchley Road where it would join the Metropolitan on the surface and take over some of its services. As we shall see, the services it actually got were not those originally earmarked.

The next scheme was the Northern. This was regarded as the most urgent. It involved the extension of the Great Northern and City Line north from Finsbury Park over existing lines owned by the London & North Eastern Railway to Alexandra Palace, High Barnet and Edgware. The Morden-Edgware Line was to be extended from Archway to East Finchley to give a connection with the LNER lines. A further extension north from Edgware to Elstree was also included later.

The last of the four schemes was the North Eastern. This, like the Northern, also involved taking over the passenger services of LNER branches; in this case, the Loughton, Ongar and Hainault lines which were to be connected to the Central Line via eastern extensions from Liverpool Street to Leytonstone and Newbury Park.

Each of these schemes required new rolling stock. As each was an extension of an existing line, the numbers of new cars required were calculated on the numbers of peak hour passengers expected divided by car carrying capacity. In addition, a large number of cars needed replacing. The Central Line, at this time still referred to as the Central London, the name of the original owning company, had 256 cars built between 1900 and 1915. Although these cars had been rebuilt in 1926-28 they were wooden-bodied, slow and old fashioned and needed replacement. The GN&C line also had a small fleet of 76 cars which were mostly over 30 years old in 1933 and many of which, like the Central stock, had wooden bodies. These were also to be replaced under the 1935-40 New Works Programme.

The replacement of the old Central London stock was already under consideration by the Underground group in 1933 and the process was carried on by the LPTB. It presented a particular problem in that the Central's tunnels were slightly smaller than a standard tube tunnel and would not accommodate tube cars of the type running on the Bakerloo, Piccadilly and Morden-Edgware lines. It was therefore necessary to design a 'compact' version of a standard car. This was done by early in 1934 and a mock-up of the proposed design was erected in Acton Works in the form of part of a car. At this point a new factor was introduced which was to have a profound effect on the New Works Programme. This was the question of line capacity.

For some years before the formation of the LPTB there had been problems with line capacity on the Morden-Edgware and Bakerloo lines and, following the extension of Piccadilly line services to Uxbridge, Hounslow and Cockfosters in 1932-3, there was a sharp increase in traffic on that line to the extent that its capacity in the central area was also being stretched. While plans for new works were being drawn up, the question of line capacity was investigated and, as an initial proposal, train lengthening was put forward. For the Morden-Edgware Line, where the problem was already serious, it was proposed to lengthen 33 of the existing trains from 7 to 8 cars for certain peak-hour workings by buying 33 new cars, plus 2 spares, to make up the numbers of cars needed. Platform lengthening, resignalling and siding lengthening was included in the expected cost of £1.25 million. It was suggested that similar schemes would

be needed for lengthening 6-car trains on the Bakerloo and Central lines to 8 cars.

The Morden-Edgware scheme was expensive. It involved lengthening 90 platform faces, mostly in tunnel and it was considered that, at best, it would only be enough to overcome the existing overcrowding. It left no room for future traffic increases which were expected when the planned extensions opened. A re-appraisal of the situation, including a closer look at the new rolling stock design, led to a new proposal which was submitted by J.P. Thomas, the General Manager (Railways) of the LPTB, in February 1936.

The new proposal was simple. Instead of equipping the Central Line with new cars as had originally been proposed, the new cars were to go to the Morden-Edgware Line and the existing Standard cars on the Morden-Edgware Line, 780 in total, would go on the Central. The new cars, which were to have all their equipment under the floor giving better passenger capacity and better traction and braking performance, were expected to increase the line capacity at peak periods by 20%.

At the same time, it was proposed to proceed with the scheme to lengthen all Central Line platforms from 6-car to 8-car capacity. Instead of the 90 platforms of the Morden-Edgware Line, only 30 Central Line platforms had to be done. This was obviously more economical but there was still one drawback. As mentioned above the Central London tunnels were too small to take Standard tube stock. They would have to be widened. This, however, was a better long term investment than having to build a special, reduced-size stock every 35 years and it gave an added advantage in giving room at the track level for the standard Underground 4-rail current supply system to be installed in place of the existing 3-rail Central London system with its centre positive rail.

A further benefit of the new plan was that the Morden-Edgware Line would have only one type of stock. If new stock were to be ordered for the Alexandra Palace, High Barnet and Elstree extensions only, it would have to work over the existing line with standard stock. New stock therefore would either have to be a repeat order for Standard stock, which would allow complete interchangeability, or it would be to the latest design and be unable to work with the old cars. Running new, high performance cars with older, slower cars was to be avoided if at all possible. The new plan virtually solved this problem and with the other benefits described above convinced the LPT Board that they should give it their blessing. This they did, in March 1936, but provisional upon their approval of the new stock prototype, of which they had so far only seen a design outline, and which was on order at this time.

As it turned out, the plan to work the Morden-Edgware and its extensions – henceforth known as the Northern Line – with all new cars did not quite work out and other events were to take over completely with the outbreak of the Second World War in September 1939. During this time also, the Bakerloo was programmed for alterations to its platforms to allow the running of 8-car trains, but this was also changed and the new stock delivery programme altered as a result.

Modern Wonder

TWOPENCE·
EVERY WEDNESDAY
Vol. 3. No. 66. Week ending August 20, 1938

LONDON'S STREAMLINED TUBE TRAIN

There are four of these trains made up of six cars each and developing 1,656 h.p., running on 600 volts D.C. They have greater acceleration and braking power and are now in service on the Piccadilly Line.

A great feature is that all the control gear and motors, etc., are beneath the floor, thus giving greater seating capacity. The rail clearance to do this is only sixteen inches.

1. Section through London clay
2. Concrete lining 3. Section of steel tunnel
4. Asbestos-lined tunnel to eliminate noise
5, 5A. Electric windscreen wipers
6. Driver's loud-speaker
7. Tunnel lighting unit for workmen
8. Tunnel lighting cable 9. Telephone cables
10. Automatic signal cables 11. Power cable
12. Hand-rail 13. Brake gauges
14. Electro-pneumatic brake handle

15. Automatic air brake handle
16. Joy-stick control 17. Automatic coupling
18, 18A. Live rails 19. Insulator
20. Concrete foundation for track
21. Face-plate controller
22, 22A. Contact shoes 23. Air reservoir
24. Power bogie 25. Brake cylinder and shoe
26. 138 h.p. traction motor 27. Driving gears
28. Extra space for passengers instead of the old motor-room

Cover of 'Modern Wonder' magazine dated 20th August 1938. The streamlined stock no doubt made for a more impressive front picture but had been superseded by this time by the flat-ended design.

As we have seen, the planning for the New Works Programme began very shortly after the formation of the LPTB in 1933. When the planners began looking at rolling stock requirements for the extensions early in 1934, the most recently available design of tube car was used in calculating the actual number of new cars required. The design used was in the 1931 Standard stock, introduced for the Piccadilly Line extensions to Hounslow, Uxbridge and Cockfosters. As we shall see, the calculations eventually proved wrong, both as to number needed and their cost but, initially, 1164 cars were suggested at a cost of £3750 each. The number of cars was broken down into the four New Works areas as follows:

Northern extensions and replacement of 76 GN&C cars	305 cars
North Eastern extensions of Central and replacement of 256 CLR cars	629 cars
Western extension of Central to Denham	100 cars
North Western extension of Bakerloo over Met Line	130 cars
Total	1164 cars

It is interesting to see how these figures were arrived at. In the cases of the Northern and both the Central Line allocations, run times, service intervals and the number of cars required to operate them were based on the 1931 Standard stock's performance. A total of 1034 cars was envisaged as being necessary. The remaining 130 cars were to be for the extension of the Bakerloo services.

The proposed Bakerloo extensions were the result of a number of interesting proposals formulated during the late 1920s and early 1930s. The whole basis of the plans was the relief of the bottleneck which existed between Finchley Road and Baker Street. The four-track Metropolitan Railway main line narrowed to two tracks south of Finchley Road and caused a daily peak-hour throttling of the Metropolitan's service to Baker Street and the City. During the 1920s the Metropolitan considered several schemes to relieve the bottleneck and in 1926 obtained powers for a relief line from Finchley Road to Edgware Road. This was still 'on the cards' when the Met was absorbed into London Transport in 1933. The scheme was altered in 1934 to become a new tube line starting from Finchley Road to a junction with the existing Bakerloo at Baker Street. Bakerloo trains would take some of the traffic from the Metropolitan and ease the congestion. It would also give a new direct route from the Metropolitan Line to the west end of London.

In its original version the Bakerloo service over the Met Line was to have consisted of an express service from Finchley Road to Harrow-on-the-Hill, stopping only at Wembley Park. Ten Bakerloo trains per hour were to be provided in the peaks with another ten serving Stanmore. The 130 cars allocated to the Bakerloo extension were to be of a new 'High Speed Tube Train' type. The idea for the Bakerloo service to Harrow was abandoned however, because it would have required a reduction in the service to Queens Park.

In a 1934 memo to the Chief Mechanical Engineer, W.A. Agnew (who had held equivalent posts since 1906 and who was due to retire in a few months time) W.S. Graff-Baker, his deputy, wrote, 'The high speed train is at present designed to carry 50 seated passengers per car in Green Line Coach type seating and has two 3ft 3ins side sliding doors . . . with two small motors under every car . . .'. Graff-Baker was in charge of new car design at this time and the designs for all the new cars built during this period – both tube and surface – were largely his. Here, in these few words, was the genesis of the 1938 Tube Stock design.

However, the tantalising prospect of all-motor-car, high speed tube trains was somewhat dampened in a further note written by Graff-Baker in August 1934, 'If these trains are to be used extensively on short-section intensive working it will be necessary to increase the doors to at least 4ft 6ins each with a reduction in seating to a maximum of 46 per car.' Slowly, the 1938 stock we came to know was beginning to appear. However whilst the concept of a 'high speed' train on the Met Line was reasonable, the idea of its use on the busy section of the Bakerloo south of Baker Street through Oxford Circus to Waterloo was questionable to say the least and, eventually the whole 'high speed' Bakerloo idea was dropped. The plans were altered in June 1935 so that the stopping service over the Met north of Finchley Road was to be provided by Bakerloo trains and they would work through to Stanmore during peak periods. When the new services actually began Stanmore was given an all-day service of Bakerloo trains to the west end. The Metropolitan continued to work all the 'express' services.

The concept of the high-speed tube train, while lost as far as an express Bakerloo service was concerned, remained as the basis for future tube car body design. Graff-Baker wanted to build a 'sample' train, as he called it, to test certain new design concepts, mainly various versions of small sized motors, control gear and auxiliary equipment. By January 1935, preliminary designs for it were complete and six cars were ordered from Metro-Cammell of Birmingham in the May of that year. This was the first of the 1935 experimental tube stock.

The 1935 Tube Stock

Graff-Baker had already been dabbling with his design for a high speed tube train for a number of years. He had persuaded his chief, W.A. Agnew, to let him try a number of experiments with a view to incorporating the ideas in his new train. He proposed a number of radical changes to existing body and equipment design. The electrical equipment was to be fit below the car floor, instead of being housed in a compartment behind the cab as on previous tube cars. The car ends were to be streamlined, as was the fashion in vogue then. The cars were to be arranged into semi-permanently coupled pairs with shared auxiliary equipment. This prevented them working alone as had been possible with earlier cars – they had to run as a pair. Pairs, or 'units' were to be coupled together with fully automatic couplers to form trains instead of the individual, manually coupled Standard cars. Further proposals included a pressure ventilated body built on a welded steel underframe resting on welded frame trucks.

To test some of these proposals, a number of trials were carried out on existing cars, one of which involved the fitting of a streamlined cab to a 1923-built Metro-Carriage Wagon & Finance Co. control trailer car, No. 1755. This work was completed in January 1933 and the car took part in several trial runs between Hammersmith and Finsbury Park on the Piccadilly Line on the night of Sunday/Monday 30th April/1st May 1933. The test train was formed of Driving Motor–Control Trailer–Control Trailer–Driving Motor + experimental Control Trailer. The experimental car was located at its east end. In July 1933 the experimental cab end was removed and the car reverted to a normal Control Trailer.

Another experiment took place with Tomlinson automatic couplers, first tried out on 1928 UCC-built Control Trailers 5012 and 5046 on the Piccadilly Line in 1933. The experimental couplers were the forerunners of the Wedglock automatic coupler, common to all Underground passenger rolling stock today. The two cars fitted with Tomlinson couplers were able to couple mechanically, electrically and pneumatically, and had 32 electrical circuits and two air connections. The electrical contacts were mounted in two groups on either side of the coupler face. The mechanical coupling of the cars was done by impact and the electrical and pneumatic connections were made by pushing a button in the cab.

Tomlinson was an American rolling stock engineer who had been concerned with providing multiple unit operation between tramcars in Boston, Massachusetts, USA. Although it was reasonably satisfactory, his coupler was too light in construction for railway work as opposed to tramway work and, following a breakaway on Ealing Common bank, it was taken out of passenger service. However, the tests persuaded Graff-Baker to pursue a design which would be suitable for the Underground and he succeeded in getting Messrs G.D. Peters of Slough to take on the research and development in return for a promise that they would, if successful, receive a very large order for the device. Accordingly, late in 1934, Peters couplers were fitted to two 1927 MCW Trailers on the Bakerloo (Nos. 1944 and 5151).

Another interesting experiment took place in late 1934, when 1927 MCW Trailer car 7195 was fitted with air conditioning equipment. The main aim of this experiment was really to reduce the amount of noise created in tube cars, with the air conditioning following on from that, as all windows and ventilator openings were sealed up. This included the roof ventilators, the ventilators above the communicating doors and the drop windows in the communicating doors. The main car windows were double-glazed. The air conditioning equipment was supplied by Frigidaire Ltd, with most of it being placed underneath the car. Cool air was blown into the car via a cowl running along the centre of the car ceiling. The car entered Acton Works in September 1934 as car 1225 from the Bakerloo Line. It was converted, overhauled and renumbered 7195 in December 1934, and was transferred to the Morden-Edgware Line on 15th December 1934, on which line it ran in service, but only for a short period, covering only 4,896 miles up to mid-April 1935. It did not run again in passenger service in that form, returning to the Bakerloo on 5th November 1935 having been converted back to normal.

A crucial part of Graff-Baker's new design was to get all the electrical equipment under the floor and he persuaded one motor manufacturer, Crompton-Parkinson, to try a small-motor design project. As part of this work, he converted the floor of a Standard trailer car so that it was raised 4ins over the bogies and had a 2ft x 2ft ramp at each end. The ramps and raised area fitted between the longitudinal seats and were just high enough to clear the motor casing below. As eventually designed for the 1935 and 1938 cars, the raised areas were extended into the doorways and they became a hallmark of tube car design until the mid-1960s.

1923 Standard stock control trailer No.1755 with a streamlined front end fitted to test the idea prior to its introduction on the 1935 experimental tube stock. It is seen here early in 1933 in Ealing Common depot.

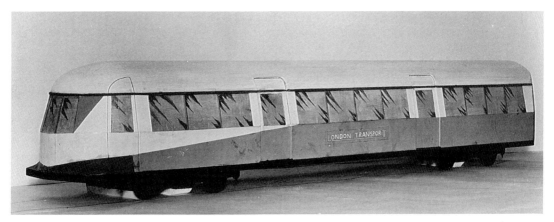

A model of the 1935 experimental tube stock as shown to Underground managers in January 1935. It had only two, single-leaf doors, per side. As built the stock had two double doors and a single door at the end. The cream flash at the front was rejected as being too garish. LUL

Before the final design for the 1935 stock was settled, various models and mock-ups were constructed; one plan was to have single-leaf passenger doors, two down each side of the car with no end single doors at the trailing end. Plans were also drawn up for an enlarged streamlined car which would fit inside a 13ft 6in tunnel. The new tunnel size was proposed for a series of high-speed, deep level tube lines to be built under London. These plans were still on the drawing board when the Underground was taken over in 1933 by the London Passenger Transport Board.

Immediately after came the plans for the 1935-40 New Works Programme. The High Speed Stock, Long Distance Tube Cars or New Suburban Stock as it was variously called by this time, was integrated into the 1935-40 New Works Programme as the prototype for the new tube stock. On 16th January 1935, Graff-Baker submitted a paper to the Engineering Committee of the LPTB which together with a sketch and a photograph of a model, described the design of the new train.

'These cars are designed to run in pairs permanently coupled together, the outer ends of the two-car unit being streamlined and the streamlined ends used as a driver's and/or guard's compartment.

'Such an arrangement contemplates trains made up of 2, 4, 6 or 8 cars. If, however, odd numbers are required, there would be no difficulty in inserting between two cars of the type illustrated a third car which would have two square ends and no driver's compartment, the seating capacity of such a car being some six seats more than the end cars, thus improving on . . . the weight-per-seat-per-run figures . . .'.

With this idea he had introduced the concept of the non-driving motor car. He envisaged all trains having all motor cars. He went on . . .'The speed characteristics of a train made up of this type of car are that it will maintain a maximum speed on level tangent track of 70 miles an hour and a speed of 60 miles an hour up a gradient of 1 in 100. Owing to their higher acceleration such trains would also be capable of improving on the performance of the present 7-car tube trains on short sections, being able to maintain the present

timing over the half-mile section with a maximum speed not exceeding 30 miles an hour against the present figure of 32 miles an hour. The higher acceleration is rendered possible by the wider distribution of motive power, each car being provided with two motors, one on each bogie. These motors are, of course, smaller than the motors normally used on our rolling stock and the car is so contrived that by raising the floor level inside the passenger compartment 4ins at each end the motors can be accommodated under the floor, together with the necessary control equipment, thus avoiding the waste space inseparable from the present arrangement of large motors and an equipment compartment . . .

'Each car is provided with two doorways per side having a 4ft 6ins clear opening with a distance of 5ft 3ins between the windscreens.' He had only two doorways per side at this stage. This is surprising – after all, the 1931 tube trailer cars had four doorways per car side. One suspects that, at first, he was cautious about having a large number of openings in a body carrying traction equipment and subject to the stresses of traction motors mounted underneath. Later he put in a 2ft 3ins doorway at all the non-driving ends. 'To keep out noise the glazing on the side of the car is double, the pillars being placed between the glasses. The centre of the car is occupied by cross-seats which can be arranged in various manners, the cross-seats in question being of the same general type as those which are in use on our long distance Green Line coaches. Further cross-seats are provided at the trailing end of each car and the remaining seats, also having Green Line characteristics as far as possible, are longitudinal seats owing to the necessity for providing space for the wheels. The total seating capacity of the car is 46,' (the extra doorways later reduced this to 40) 'or an average of .86 seats per foot run of train, as compared with the present condition on a 7-car train of .7 per foot run.

'The bogies have a wheelbase of 6ft 3in unequally distributed about the centre in the ratio of 2ft 9in to 3ft 6in, the 3ft 9in end carrying the motor, thus getting a certain degree of maximum traction effect.

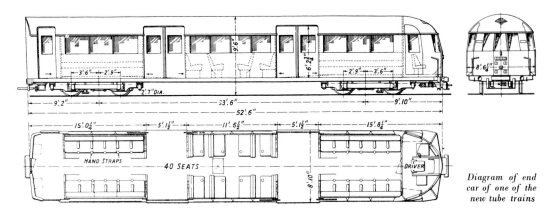

Diagram of end car of one of the new tube trains

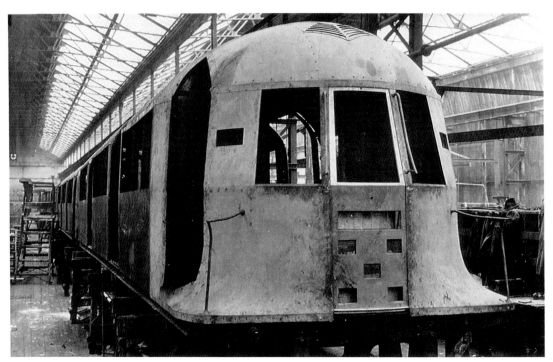

1935 streamlined experimental tube cars under construction at Metro-Cammell's works in Birmingham. LURS collection

'The bolster is suspended by inclined bolster hangers of considerable length spaced at 5ft 6ins centres, compared with the normal tube bogie bolster suspension which has links at about 4ft 4ins centres. The increased distance is known to be effective in giving better riding, and the bogie frame is designed to accommodate a long bolster to meet this requirement.' This gave rise to the now famous bay-window side frame shape of the bogie.

'The bogie is constructed entirely by welding methods so far as the structural parts are concerned.' This was to be a source of much trouble in later years.

'The car as designed contemplates the elimination of ventilating windows or roof ventilators in order to obtain the quietest possible running, and to meet this fact and to provide a satisfactory atmosphere under all circumstances it is necessary to adopt the use of air conditioning apparatus. The air in the car will be recirculated and cooled or warmed during this recirculation, with a view to keeping a satisfactory temperature and reducing the moisture content of the air which is the chief cause of discomfort in a crowded car.

'In order to provide ventilation ducts between the apparatus on the underframe and the interior of the car, the windscreens at the door side are made of double glass, the space between being used for distributing the air. In addition, narrow vertical trunks are provided at the ends of the passenger compartments.'

The ducts were to be similar to those fitted to the Metadyne equipped 'O' stock built at this time for the Hammersmith and City Line but in fact were omitted from the tube cars as built.

'The car and bogie are designed with a view to the adoption, in so far as may be advantageous, of autogenous welding and light drawn sections. It is assumed that such a car would naturally be fitted with fully automatic couplings, making air and electrical connections as well as the drawbar engagement.

'The doors would be air operated and the circuits for the doors and all auxiliary purposes including lighting, but excluding heating, would be at 50 volts provided by a motor generator set. It is considered that a 50-volt system for control and door operation would be less prone to trouble, and 50-volt lighting results in a higher efficiency lamp with a probable increase in life. The 50-volt system would have an earth return and batteries would be provided to cover emergencies and any temporary interruption of the current supply when passing over gaps.

'The control gear would have 60 notches for smooth acceleration and four economical running points according to whether high speed or short section operation were required, and means would be provided to prevent very high speeds being attainable in tunnel conditions, or the train exceeding a set speed downhill.'

How this was to be done is not clear. The 'means' did not appear on the train. Neither did it attain 'very high speeds', at least not in today's terms.

'The driver's compartment is provided with swing doors at each side for the use of the guard and for access of the motorman, while the motorman is provided with an adjustable armchair type of seat situated at the approximate optical centre of the streamlined end. A communication door is provided in the end of the car and, owing to the shape of the end, this door has to be made to slide bodily backwards on rollers along the longitudinal centre line of the car. This appears to offer no difficulty and has the great advantage of being made much more readily draught-proof than any other form of swing or lateral sliding door. The brakes would be of the self-lapping electro-pneumatic type which gives a braking effort proportional to the position of the handle, thus eliminating the position time element factor of the present brakes. The brake and traction controllers would be operated by lever arms at each side of the driver's seat. The three front windows of the car would be fitted with windscreen wipers.

'The streamlined ends are at the present time subject to investigations as to the dynamic advantages that may be gained, but apart from any advantages, which anyway are not likely to be apparent under 45 miles per hour, it is suggested that the present times demand some appearance of the kind.'

'This type of car is essentially different from any car that has yet been constructed for electric traction, having in mind particularly the restricted space available in a tube tunnel. It must therefore be regarded at the present time as experimental, and it is suggested that it would be wise to construct a pair, or more, of such cars for trial purposes to prove the performance and amenities of the vehicles.'

Graff-Baker thought of streamlining as a sop to fashion and doubted (rightly) its value on an Under-ground train. The Engineering Committee didn't like it either and decided to withhold their approval of Agnew's request, as Graff-Baker's chief, for £25,496 to be spent on a 2-car prototype train. They used the raised floor experiment as their excuse, wanting to see it themselves before proceeding further. Frank Pick, the LPTB Vice-Chairman, also hated the broad cream 'flash' which appeared on the side of the model. He, and others, criticised the appearance of the rounded ends in the middle coupling points as well.

Four months elapsed before a renewed submission was made. This time, Graff-Baker was his own boss, Agnew having retired after almost 30 years as CME, and he had done some homework.

'Approximate figures recently obtained,' he wrote in his submission of 15th May, 'show that the total cost of 6-car train (in quantities) would be £33,400 compared with £25,000 for an existing standard 7-car tube train. £5,200 of this increased cost is due to the provision of air conditioning or otherwise ventilating the cars, the provision of fully automatic couplers, and the fitting of self-lapping brakes. It is considered that these should all be retained at least in an experiment. There are certain savings with the new cars to offset the extra cost. For instance, to use a known basis, consider the present service on the Hampstead Line where 99 trains are now in service. A saving of 4 trains could be given on the line if it were re-equipped with the new type car. The financial advantage of the new train would work out then as follows:

Saving of 4 trains in capital cost
= 4 x £25,000 = £100,000
or per train on remaining 95 trains = £1,050
Saving of operating costs @ £2,900 per
train on 4 trains = £11,600
Capitalised at 5% – £232,000
or per train on 95 trains   = £2,440
                                       £3,490 per train total.

'It will thus be seen that the additional cost is either accounted for by increased operating facilities or passenger amenities or offset by savings in operating expenses and interest charges.'

After this, and more on the cost saving by not having to lengthen platforms if new type trains were used, the Committee, and later the Board, could hardly refuse him. He actually asked for, and got, £50,000 for a complete 6-car train, substantially as described above, but with the extra end doorways.

The High Speed Train Arrives

The formal request was submitted to the Board on 30th May 1935 for the expenditure of £50,000 on an experimental 6-car high speed tube train. The request was approved and the order for the car bodies was placed with Metropolitan-Cammell soon afterwards. The train, consisting of six motor cars with streamlined (sometimes later called 'bull-nosed') cab ends, was made up of three 2-car units which were delivered to the depot at Lillie Bridge in October and November 1936, and then transferred to Ealing Common depot for commissioning.

This and Facing Page **The first two-car streamlined 1935 stock unit, 10000-11000, at Northfields depot, Ealing Common depot and on the test track between South Ealing and Acton Town in November 1936.** LUL

The electrical equipment was ordered from Allen West and Cromptons (who were commercially connected) after Graff-Baker had persuaded them to re-enter the railway traction field. The other three major traction equipment manufacturers, GEC, BTH, and Metropolitan Vickers, promptly shouted 'foul' and the orders for the new train were quickly expanded to a total of 24 cars to give four 6-car trains, the three additional ones equipped by these companies. The last train was partially redesigned to eliminate the hated streamlined ends and each train was to have equipment by different manufacturers.

The cars were numbered 10000-11, 11000-11011. They were formed into 2-car units of similarly numbered pairs. Units 10000-11000 to 10008-11008 were those built with the streamlined driving cab ends, while 10009-11009 to 10011-11011 had the flat-fronted cabs, the design of which was subsequently adopted for the main 1938 tube stock fleet.

The first known test run took place on Monday 13th November 1936, on the test tracks between Acton Town and Northfields, during the midday off-peak period, and tests continued on most Mondays to Fridays until 8th January 1937, excluding the Christmas holiday period. On 17th November 1936, a train was made available to the press in Northfields depot for inspection. This was widely reported in the London evening newspapers on 17th November, and the national newspapers the following day. One newspaper optimistically forecast that with these trains, the days of 'straphanging' would be over, while another described the train as 'a streamlined wonder'. Nearly all the newspaper reports had photographs of the train and carried extensive descriptions of it. The outstanding features picked up by the press were: air conditioning, quieter and smoother rides, and quick acceleration (2mph per second). The three London evening papers reported that heated grab poles were provided, but no evidence can be found to confirm this.

As originally ordered the first train was given a special classification system, based on the then existing scheme used to identify the direction in which cars faced. Driving cars were classified 'A' if they faced west, or 'B' if they faced east. Each of the three units of this experimental train therefore had an 'A' car and a 'B' car. Each unit was also classified 'A' (cars 10000-11000), 'B' (cars 10001-11001) and 'C' (cars 10002-11002). This notation was altered from March 1937 when a new system was introduced where car axles were lettered A, B, C, and D and the end of the car nearest the 'A' axle became the 'A' end, and the end nearest the 'D' axle, the 'D' end. Cars with the cab at the 'A' end remained 'A' cars but the 'B' cars became 'D' cars. The A, B, and C notation used for the first three units delivered was abandoned at this time and was only applied to the other three trains while they were under construction at Metro-Cammell's using the letters D to M (excluding I).

When the cars arrived at Ealing Common depot each of the contractors supplying the various equipments had staff on site to put the finishing touches and arrange acceptance tests. Apart from the MV equipped train, which ran as four cars, all acceptance tests were done on their own as two-car units. After extensive tests the first of the new trains entered passenger service on 8th April 1937 on the Piccadilly Line. The others followed at various times until the last on 10th March 1938.

When new, the trains were scheduled to work on specified workings only on Mondays to Fridays. Initially, these workings were changed at regular intervals, sometimes week by week, but all started after the morning peak as four-car trains and stabled before the evening peak started. From 26th April 1937, however, the afternoon workings coupled up in service to form six-car trains, working right through the evening peak. The coupling was performed in the eastbound platform at Northfields, with the extra two-car unit starting from Northfields depot.

A second timetable path for an experimental train began from 24th January 1938 on Mondays to Fridays, and was used by four cars of the flat-fronted type. However, this working was short-lived as units 10009-11009 + 10010-11010 were transferred to the Northern Line for gauging purposes prior to the arrival of the 1938 tube stock, which had by then been ordered. They were transferred to Golders Green on 31st March 1938 and returned to the Piccadilly Line on 4th July 1938. The flat-fronted units were chosen for gauging as their dimensions were almost identical to the 1938 tube stock.

Above **Interior of driver's cab of GEC equipped unit. On the left is the brake controller joystick and on the right, that for power. Under the right hand window is the speedometer and above the door the special shunting buttons for use when coupling.** GEC

Right **A view under a GEC equipped car showing, in the foreground, the negative shoe and, behind it, the multi-notch camshaft control equipment. As is obvious from this photograph, space was at a premium.** GEC

The last train of 1935 stock was built with flat ends. It was the true prototype for the 1938 stock. Unit 10009-11009 is seen here at Northfields depot late in 1937. LT Museum

1935 stock car 10010 in Ealing Common depot under preparation for service. Note that even the roof had a gloss finish and that, in accordance with the paint scheme shown on the model, the tops of the doors were painted grey to match the roof. It appears that the streamlined cars were done in the same way. LT Museum

A third train became available for service on the Piccadilly Line from 2nd August 1938. When all units had been in service for some months, four paths were made available in the timetable, although it was very rare for them all to be utilised. The duty which stabled at Northfields after the morning peak was the one invariably used, because there was nobody at Cockfosters trained to deal with defects and, if there was a problem with it, the train would have to return empty to Northfields.

By this time, the production version of the new stock was already being delivered. The first cars arrived at Lillie Bridge in May 1938. The orders for these cars were, however, quite different from those first envisaged back in 1934. At that time, the total of 1164 new cars proposed for the extensions was based on the specification for Standard stock. With the decision to go ahead with the 'high speed' design in May 1935 and a subsequent appraisal of the rolling stock requirements, new figures for each new Works extension were worked out as follows:

	Total of Cars Required		
Scheme	New	Old	+ or −
Northern extensions and replacement of 76 GN&C cars	233	305	− 72
North Eastern extension of Central and replacement of 256 CLR cars	585	629	− 44
Western extension of Central to Denham	96	100	− 4
North Western extension of Bakerloo	130	130	
Totals	1044	1164	− 120

There was a saving of 120 cars over the 1934 estimate. Of course, this was not without a serious drawback. The new cars were now estimated to cost £5000 each, £1250 over the original estimate of 1934, or roundly 30% more. This was, in part, compensated for by the reduced numbers, by the increased capacity and by the improvement in performance expected, as Graff-Baker had explained in his submission of May 1935. Also, the design would have the latest technology and it was thought, would be bound to encourage traffic. All in all, it seemed the right thing to do. In the meantime, some further developments led to another appraisal of the numbers of cars required.

The original 'New Works' plans to extend the former Great Northern & City Line north to join up with the LNER lines to Edgware, High Barnet and Alexandra Palace and to connect them to the Hampstead and City Line tube at Highgate, did not include any plans to go north of Edgware. However, the area north of Edgware had always been a prime target for Underground expansion ever since the First World War when the extension of Bakerloo services to Watford (LNWR, later LMS) had proved the long-distance capability of the tube system. As we have seen, in 1923 St Albans was earmarked as the northern terminus of a vast Bakerloo-Hampstead expansion scheme and the route via Edgware had always figured highly in the company's plans. The 1935-40 programme however had specifically excluded the route because of doubts about the ability of the existing in-town section of the line to carry any more traffic – it was overcrowded as it was, hence the suggestions of platform lengthening. Eventually though, the LPTB was forced to consider a further northern extension, not because of a desire for more traffic but because of a shortage of depot accommodation.

Under the new Northern line scheme, the existing depots at Golders Green and Morden would not have been capable of carrying out the maintenance of the enlarged fleet planned for the line. A search for ways of enlarging the maintenance facilities was begun and it quickly became clear that no further space was available for expansion at the existing depots. Even with the addition of Drayton Park depot on the GN&C line, there was not enough room. The only solution was a new depot.

Suitable sites were now looked at. One was at Finchley Manor, near where the LNER High Barnet line passed under the North Circular Road and where it was proposed there should be a new station. Another was at Copthall Park, the land for which had just been purchased by Hendon Borough Council. However, it

was found that the Finchley Manor site was too small and the Copthall Park site, although big enough, would not be released by Hendon Council. The only alternative site was near the proposed route north of Edgware to Elstree. As some land for the line had already been acquired a few years before and the site was really the only suitable one available, the Elstree extension suddenly became part of the New Works Programme and, in October 1936, it was calculated that 16 additional cars were needed to work services on the extension.

At first the 16 additional cars were simply added to the existing total of 1044 to give 1060 new cars to be ordered. However a considerable amount of juggling was done – first with the figures for expected patronage on the extensions, then with the numbers of new cars needed for each of the four New Works schemes and then with their financial allocations so that, by the late summer of 1936, new totals had been drawn up as follows:

Scheme	Total of Cars required			
	Orig.	Old	New	+ or –
Northern extensions and replacement of 76 GN&C cars	305	233	245	(+12)
North Eastern extension of Central and replacement of 256 CLR cars	629	585	551	(-34)
Western extension of Central to Denham	100	96	76	(-20)
North Western extension of Bakerloo over Met Line	130	130	162	(+32)
Elstree			16	(+16)
Totals	1164	1044	1050	(+ 6)

The new allocations reflected two new schemes. One was the Elstree extension, the other was the decision to increase all Bakerloo trains to 7-cars instead of six. The original plan for the Bakerloo envisaged increasing the length of all platforms to take 8-car trains but

Front end view and interior view of 1935 stock flat-ended car looking towards the cab. This car has conventional tilting vents. Note the slope of the floor at the doorway. LT Museum

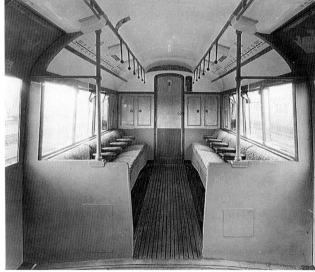

this was later reduced to 7-cars on the now familiar grounds that if new cars were used they would give increased capacity. However, originally only 16 trains were to have seven cars; the rest were to remain 6-cars, including 10 then running on the Bakerloo with 1920 built Cammell-Laird trailers.

Under the revised plans these ten trains were to be reformed with the 1920 trailers being replaced by Standard tube stock ones and lengthened to seven cars. All other trains were also to become seven cars, thus increasing the Bakerloo allocation of new cars by 32. This was achieved by reducing the Central Line by 54 cars by reducing the length of some rush hour trains from eight cars to seven. After 32 had gone to the Bakerloo and 12 to the Northern to boost that line's allocation, there were still 10 left over. These were used for Elstree which now needed only six new cars to be added to the total to be purchased.

The 40 displaced Cammell Laird cars remained a problem. They were only 15 years old but they were old-fashioned compared with Standard stock and positively archaic compared with 1938 stock. Eventually it was decided they should be used on the Finsbury Park-Moorgate shuttle service planned for the Northern City Line when the extensions were opened. They were to be formed into 6-car trains with two Standard stock motor cars, much as they had been on the Bakerloo. As only 16 of them were needed, the other 24 cars were to be scrapped or used as service vehicles.

So far, the allocation of new cars was simply on a financial basis. As we have seen, there was no intention to run the new stock on the Central Line. It was to run only on the Northern and Bakerloo.

Train and Car Allocations

Now is perhaps the point at which to consider the types of new cars and how they were to be allocated. It will then become clear how the cars ordered fitted into the New Works Programme. After all, the amount of money available for new cars was limited by the financing of the Programme and some careful balancing of car allocations was needed to get the best out of what was available.

The basic 7-car Standard tube stock formation was as follows: M-T-T-M+CT-T-M, i.e. motor-trailer-trailer-motor + control trailer-trailer-motor. A 6-car set could be made up of two motors at each end of four trailers or control trailers as required. Shorter trains of 3-(M-T-CT) or 4-(M-T-T-M) cars could be formed if needed. All these formations were used on the Bakerloo, Piccadilly and Northern Lines to a greater or lesser extent.

Graff-Baker's original plan for the 1935 experimental train had been for 6-car or 7-car all-motored formations. Mindful of the problems this was likely to cause the current supply system, not to mention the signal overlaps, he later diluted each formation with a trailer car. He also eliminated some of the unnecessary middle cabs by using a 4-car unit instead of 2 x 2-car units. He also, much to everyone's relief, got rid of the streamlined cab end.

The new 1938 stock was therefore designed to work as 3-car, 4-car or 7-car trains but, unlike the Standard stock, it could not readily be broken down into individual cars. The cars making up a 3-car or 4-car unit were semi-permanently coupled and could only be split up in a workshop. A pair of 3-car units or a 3-car plus a 4-car could, however, be coupled or uncoupled easily in service as the driving ends of the units had fully-automatic couplers.

There were to be three types of unit formation:

DM (Driving Motor) – NDM (Non Driving Motor) – DM
DM – T – NDM – DM
DM – T – DM

Left **A pipe-fitter's nightmare. The maze of conduit underneath one of the flat-ended 1935 stock cars.**

Right **Front end view of 1938 stock.** LT Museum

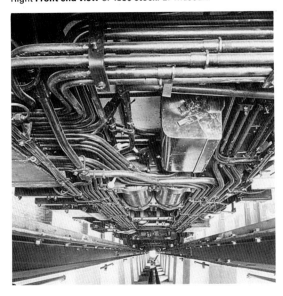

1938 tube stock in course of construction at Metro-Cammell's Midland works in Birmingham. Metro-Cammell

1938 tube stock motor cars under construction. The underframes, sides and roofs were all built separately and then erected on jigs, as seen in the background. Metro Cammell

The bogie production line at Metro-Cammell. Note how the motor wheels were spoked and the trailing wheels solid.
Metro-Cammell

The erecting shop at Old Park Works. On the left is an underframe, on the right a motor car nearing completion of erection.
Metro-Cammell

Another view of the manufacture of 1938 stock. On the right is an underframe showing how the seat risers, although part of the underframe, actually protruded through the floor. The slots for the tops of the wheels can clearly be seen, divided by the body bolsters. *Metro-Cammell*

A motor car body nearing completion at Metro-Cammell's in 1938. Note the absence of any ventilator grille over the end cab door. All cars had these when delivered, even the 1935 stock, so it may have been omitted in error from this car and rectified before delivery. *Metro-Cammell*

Top **Two pairs of motor cars of 1938 stock (10157-11157, 10158-11158) seen at Berkhampsted during their delivery journey to London on 8th June 1939.** H. Casserley

Above **A 4-car unit of 1938 tube stock, as delivered to Morden.**

The two different types of 3-car units were to allow 6-car trains of the new stock to be run. Originally it had been intended to run 6-car DM-T-DM+DM-T-DM trains on both the Northern and Bakerloo Lines as well as 7-car trains and to run 3-car-off-peak trains. However, it was realised that a 6-car train with two trailers would be underpowered, so the DM-NDM-DM unit was proposed. This allowed a 6-car DM-NDM-DM+DM-T-DM formation. Later, the attempts to run 3-car trains during the off-peak periods with only one small air compressor on board caused some problems and 4-car sets (which had two compressors) became the standard off-peak train formation.

One other factor affected the rolling stock allocat-

ions. The transfers of Standard stock cars between lines and the new 8-car Central Line train formations threw up a batch of spare Standard stock trailers. Originally, 50 were available and it was decided to absorb these into the new trains by converting them to run with 1938 tube stock. After the reallocation, when the Bakerloo trains were all increased to 7-cars, this total became 58 trailers. Although all were built as Standard stock in 1927, they were converted to run as 1938 stock by Acton Works and henceforth became part of the 1938 stock fleet. To identify them as a group type, they became known as the '58' trailers.

The allocation of the 1938 tube stock, as ordered in March 1937, was as follows:

Line	Trains	DM	NDM	T	58T	Total
					Car Allocations:	
Northern (Morden-Bushey Heath)	110x7 cars + 111 spares	504	126	251	–	881
Northern City (Moorgate-Barnet, etc)	5x6 cars + 6 spares	24	6	–	6	36
Central (Epping Shuttle)	2x2 cars + 2 spares	6	–	–	–	6
Bakerloo (Watford Service)	23x7 cars + 24 spares	107	26	–	52	185
Total of 1938 cars: 1050 (plus 58 trailers)		641	158	251	58	1108

This list shows how the 1050 cars detailed earlier were to be distributed and they were ordered from the builders on this basis. However there followed several alterations and additions and the total number of cars ordered had, by October 1938, increased to 1121. This new total still excluded the 24 cars of 1935 experimental tube stock which it was decided should be part of the new stock allocation but included 71 additional cars.

There was another change at this time too. In addition to the normal train service requirements, a number of extra cars were needed to cover regular maintenance. For standard cars this was calculated at 10% for trailers and 15% for motor cars. Originally, these were the figures also used for the 1938 stock but, during the many reappraisals of the requirements which took place, they were adjusted to 12½% worked out on a train basis rather than on a car basis.

The first 1938 train to be delivered included 11013 seen here at Golders Green for its official photographs. LT Museum

As already mentioned, there was constant juggling with the figures to try and get the best value for money as far as car use was concerned. During the 3-year period between October 1935 and October 1938, by which time the new cars were entering service, there were nine re-allocations of rolling stock for the New Works Programme. The twenty-four 1935 stock cars, the 71 additional cars ordered during 1938 and the new method of spares calculations were included in a new stock allocation of October 1938 as follows:

Item	Cars	To be Used
1)	6 1935 DMs	to give 3 x 2-car (DM-DM) units for Central Line Epping-Ongar shuttle, releasing 6 DMs for the Bakerloo.
2)	18 1935 DMs and 3 new Trailers	to form 3 x 7-car trains for use on the Piccadilly Line.
3)	20 DMs ex Northern 6 DMs ex Central 2 new DMs 7 new NDMs 14 new Trailers	to form 7 x 7-car 1938 trains to go on Bakerloo. 7 x 7-car standard stock to go to Piccadilly Line, from Bakerloo.
4)	20 new special DMs	to replace 20 DMs removed from Northern Line (item 3).
5)	20 new special NDMs	to be used with 20 special DMs (item 4) to give 10 x 9-car trains on Northern.
6)	1 new NDM 1 new DM 2 new Trailers	as spare cars on Bakerloo.
7)	1 new Trailer	as spare car on Northern.

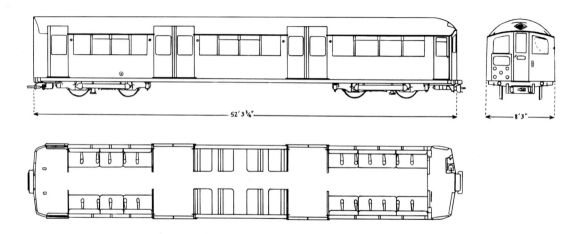

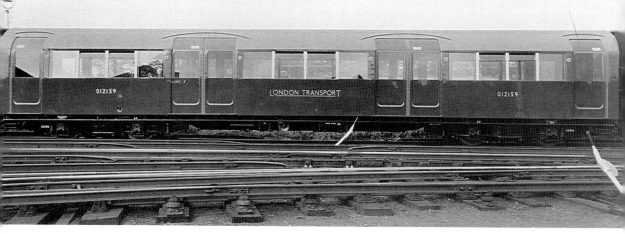

1938 tube stock trailer car in original condition. LT Museum

The net result of this was to allow a 10-train increase on the Piccadilly Line and an adjustment of the spare car allocations. The increase of the Piccadilly stock holding was as a result of the desperate situation which had arisen since the completion of the extensions to that line in 1933. The traffic levels had increased some 60% between 1934 and 1938 while the train service had only increased by 24%. As soon as enough new trains became available on the Northern Line, Standard stock began to be transferred to the Piccadilly to give some relief in time for the winter service of 1938.

Interior of 1938 trailer in original condition. LT Museum

A brand new train of 1938 stock on test at Acton Town. LT Museum

Overcrowding was not confined to the Piccadilly Line, however. We have already seen how various schemes for train lengthening were devised in an effort to relieve overcrowding on the Bakerloo and Northern, and how in March 1938 it was expected that the new stock would be sufficient to reduce the pressure. However, traffic increases continued at an unexpectedly high rate and, as early as September 1936, another scheme to increase train lengths was devised.

Nine-Car Trains

The biggest problem encountered with train lengthening schemes was always the expense of the civil engineering works necessary, particularly at tunnel stations. This was the reason why the original 9-car train idea for the Northern Line was dropped. However, a new scheme was developed during late 1936 which obviated the expensive tunnel station extensions but which still allowed limited 9-car train running during peak periods. After some night-time trial runs in mid-August 1937, an initial one-train experiment was begun on 8th November 1937 using Standard stock between Colindale and Kennington on two round trips in the morning and one round trip in the afternoon. During February 1938 the experiment was extended to Edgware with the introduction of a second train on 7th February, a third on 14th and a fourth on the 21st.

The trains were run so that, at the open stations between Edgware and Golders Green where the platforms had been specially extended, the trains would stop normally but, at the tunnel stations, they would stop with either the two leading cars or the two rear cars in the tunnel. Notices displayed on the platforms and in the trains showed which cars could be used at which stations. In theory, anyone stuck in the wrong car could walk through the train to another car to reach the platform. In practice, perhaps, some might have got carried on. However, the experiment was considered sufficiently successful for plans to be made to introduce more 9-car trains on the Northern and to plan layouts on future extensions to accommodate 9-car trains on the Central and Bakerloo Lines. Some sidings in Hainault Depot, Loughton station and Newbury Park sidings and platforms were all built to take 9-car trains. Naturally, as the Northern was about to get new stock, the 9-car trains there would have to be of this stock.

By the time the decision was taken to order more cars in August 1938, work on the original orders for 1050 cars was already well advanced. The orders had been placed in March 1937 and the first cars were delivered in May 1938. The cars ordered for the 9-car programme were added to the end of the main order and they were specially designed in order to reduce the costs.

Quite soon after the decision to have 9-car new stock trains it was decided to opt for four of them on the Golders Green-Edgware service and four on the Barnet Line, plus two spare trains. This involved increasing the length of ten 7-car trains to 9 cars each by ordering another 20 new cars. The new cars and some of the others in the trains had to be special. Because of the need to accommodate the guard's door controls within the station platforms, even with the two leading or end cars in the tunnel, these were placed on the 3rd and 7th cars. It was the usual practice to place these controls at the leading end of the rear driving car. However, they were not needed on the end driving cars of the 9-car trains so, for these 10 trains, the driving cars were special in having no door control positions. To make up for this lack, the non-driving motor cars in the third and seventh positions were also made special in being fitted with the door control positions. A 9-car train was to be formed as follows: Special DM – NDM x Special NDM – T – NDM – T – Special NDM x NDM – Special DM.

The special NDMs were fitted with guard's door controls and a handbrake, both located at the inner end of the car. At the other end of this and on the next car, also an NDM, a special coupler was fitted, marked x above. It was of the Ward type used on standard tube stock and was fitted to allow maintenance in 7-car long depot roads and for a quick emergency uncoupling in case it was necessary to stable the train (or 7 cars of it at least) in a standard 7-car length siding. The arrangement was cheaper than a pair of automatic Wedglock couplers.

The 1938 stock 9-car formation was unusual in its coupling arrangements particularly because no provision was made for breaking trains up into smaller portions for off-peak working. The third and fourth cars of a normal 7-car stock train had automatic couplers and driver's cabs to allow the train to be split into 3-car and 4-car portions for off-peak traffic. The 9-car trains were intended only for rush-hour work and were therefore made up into 'block' trains, i.e. they could only run as 9-car sets. The expense of providing cabs and couplers at intermediate points was thus saved. However, Graff-Baker commented on a debate concerning these trains, '. . . the price paid these days seems high when it is considered they run such a small mileage.' Economy was important, even then, and he was dubious about the scheme which was really an Operating Department idea pushed by J.P. Thomas.

The forming of 9-car block trains thus gave 20 spare DM cars (item 3) which were replaced by 20 new special DMs (item 4) ordered in addition to the 20 special NDMs (item 5) needed to increase ten 7-car trains to 9 cars. These spare DMs were included in the new trains formed for the Bakerloo. At the same time, the spares allocation was altered to allow all lines to have spares of 3 or 4-car units instead of individual spare cars as had been the previous practice. The final distribution of 1938 and associated stock was as follows:

Line	Service Trains	Spare Trains	Car Allocations:				
			DM	NDM	T	58T	Total
Northern (Morden-Bushey Heath)	102 x 7-cars	14 x 7-cars	464	116	232	–	812
	8 x 9-cars	2 x 9-cars	20‡	50†	20	–	90
Northern City (Moorgate-Barnet, etc)	5 x 6-cars	1 x 6-cars	24	6	–	6	36
Bakerloo	30 x 7-cars	4 x 7-cars	136	34	16	52	238
Piccadilly	2 x 7-cars	1 x 7- cars	18*	–	3‡	–	21
Central (Epping-Ongar)	2 x 2-cars	1x 2-cars	6*	–	–	–	6
			668	206	271	58	1203

Total Cars: 1938 stock: 1121 cars, 1935 stock: 25 cars, 1927 stock: 58 trailers; Total 1203.

* 1935 Stock   ‡ Special equipment
† Special equipment on 40 cars

Ordering and Delivery

When the first orders for 1938 tube stock were placed in March 1937, the planned number of cars was still 1050, divided as follows:

    641 driving motor cars from Metro-Cammell
    59 non-driving motor cars from Metro-Cammell
    99 non-driving motor cars from Birmingham
    251 trailers from Birmingham

Such large orders for car bodies, bogies, traction motors, control systems, brakes and auxiliary equipment were much sought after by suppliers and there were many hopefuls standing in the wings. The LPTB was, however, a demanding customer who expected suppliers to deliver on time, give value for money and, above all else, provide reliable equipment. To help them in their choice of contractors they retained the services of their former CME, W.A. Agnew after his retirement, to act as a consultant to help qualify tenderers.

He visited most of the major car builders in Britain during the autumn of 1936 and then prepared a short list of suitable companies. At the bottom of the list were Hurst Nelson of Motherwell and Cravens of Sheffield. He did not think them suitable for tube car work and suggested they would be suitable for service vehicles. Cravens, he noted in a memo of 14th November 1936, were a 'far oot' relation to Vickers in a reference to the financial connection between the two firms.

At the top of his list were Metro-Cammell of Birmingham, followed closely by the Birmingham Railway Carriage and Wagon Company, with Gloucester's in third place. He regarded Metro-Cammell as best for tube cars and Birmingham as adequate but said, 'I have found them a bit awkward to deal with at times'. He did not elaborate and went on to favour Gloucester for building surface line cars which, with Birmingham, they did. They got the large orders for O, P and Q stock cars.

He did go on to say, 'I cannot help thinking that – especially in the case of tube stock – the price has increased too much . . and that, with a revision of design and a rejection of several rather expensive features, you might secure substantial reductions while retaining most of the qualities of value to the Board.'

Here we see another attempt by Agnew, even after he retired, to restrain Graff-Baker's fertile and inventive mind, something he had managed to do most of the time while he was his boss at Acton. Graff-Baker had already tried to introduce all under-car equipment, more powerful trains, door fault detection systems and brake fault indicators in the mid-1920s only to have his ideas watered down or suppressed entirely by his chief. When Agnew went, Graff-Baker's schemes blossomed in the springtime of London Transport's early years. Agnew had, however, learned the hard way following the introduction of air doors during the early 1920s, that reliability was the ultimate goal even if it meant a cautious approach to new ideas. Graff-Baker was to learn the same lesson after the introduction of his new stocks in the late 1930s.

Agnew's comments about costs are interesting. In 1934, the original cost per car had been based on standard stock prices and worked out at £3750. After the new 1936 type designs had been accepted, a production run cost per car was calculated at £5200. Ultimately, the price became almost £6900 per car, although it is difficult to establish an accurate final figure now because of the intervention of the Second World War.

The first 1938 stock cars to be delivered were 10012 and its partner 11012 which were recorded as arriving at Lillie Bridge on 11th May 1938. These two cars, and five others delivered over the next two weeks, were shown to the Press on 27th June 1938 and are officially recorded as having entered service on 30th June 1938 in the formation:

10012-0123158-12000-11012 + 10013-012159-11013

This suggests that fitting of equipment, commissioning, testing, training and acceptance by the Operating Department was completed in 7 weeks. Nowadays the same process takes around 6 months! It is likely that this first train was put into service before all testing was complete because it and several of the following deliveries were withdrawn for brake cylinder modifications and were used for instruction purposes at Golders Green.

Delivery continued during the summer of 1938 with two more trains being ready in July and four in August. By this time, it had been decided to order the extra cars needed to cover the increases in the Piccadilly Line service (51 cars) and then, in the September, to order another 20 cars to allow the introduction of ten

9-car trains. The extra orders were given to both Metro-Cammell and Birmingham who now had to supply:

Metro-Cammell:	644 DMs	(increased from 641)
	107 NDMs	(increased from 59)
Birmingham:	99 NDMs	(unchanged)
	271 Trailers	(increased from 251)

By September 1938 the converted '58 trailers' began to enter service on the Northern Line, although most of them were intended for use on the Bakerloo. They were being turned out by Acton Works, where the conversion work was being done, at the rate of four a week. As the delivery of new 1938 stock was not matching this rate yet, a number of them were stored for a few weeks until the delivery of new trailers was slowed down to absorb the overflow.

By the end of November it is recorded that there were 24 new trains in service and deliveries were allowing a rate of service introduction of two trains a week. Following a gauging run on the night of December 3rd 1938, clearance was given for the new trains to run to Queens Park on the Bakerloo and the first one is recorded as entering service on 2nd January 1939 in the formation:

10044-012192-11044 + 10094-12068-11094

Although the New Works Programme called for 7-car trains on the Bakerloo, the platform lengthening programme to accommodate them had not been completed, so 6-car trains remained standard on the Bakerloo for some time to come. Also, in this first train, the use of the NDM 12068 was only temporary. It was removed and replaced by a 58 trailer early in the war to reduce the power consumption of the new stock and to match it more closely to the standard tube cars then working on the Bakerloo. This pattern was followed by subsequent Bakerloo deliveries.

At this time, the Bakerloo had not yet been connected to the Metropolitan and its trains were still being maintained at London Road. However, there were no side pits in the sheds there and these were essential for access to the equipment cases of 1938 stock. Although four trains of the stock were transferred there during January and February 1939, they were largely confined to training duties while waiting for the pits to be constructed. In addition, they could not work north of Queens Park until after 12th June 1939, the date that the LMS gave permission for the stock to work to Watford. From that date, 1938 stock began to be transferred from the Northern to the Bakerloo on a regular basis.

By 31st July 1939, there were nine 6-car 1938 stock trains on the original Bakerloo Line. There were also three 4-car trains of Standard tube stock allocated to the Metropolitan Line. These had been transferred from the Northern Line for use on the Stanmore branch. Stanmore usually had a shuttle service from Wembley Park with peak hour through trains via the Metropolitan main line to Baker Street. Pending its connection to the Bakerloo, 4-car trains of Standard stock began working on the shuttle service from time

to time. This involved raising the track to the compromise height at platforms which allowed the use of either tube or surface stock. This was completed on 26th March 1939 and Standard tube cars began working on the line from the following day.

The introduction of Standard stock on the branch was a result of the overhaul and modernisation programme being carried out at Acton Works. A huge programme of repainting, fitting of passenger door control, provision of heaters, brake equipment improvements and power enhancement was being undertaken for all the Standard stock cars being displaced from the Northern Line as 1938 tube stock was being delivered. These cars were being introduced to the Central Line as overhaul work on them was completed but the Central Line's extensions to Ruislip and Epping were a long way from complete. Some 6-car trains intended for the Central Line were used on the Bakerloo Queens Park – Elephant service from October 1938 and some overhauled cars were stored at Neasden and Stanmore. The introduction of Standard stock on the Stanmore shuttle made use of this stored stock to allow it to remain in reasonable running order. Stored railway vehicles very quickly deteriorate if not used – something of which the LPTB was fully aware and which was to cost them dearly during the war years 1940-1945.

By July 1939, the programme for overhauling cars intended for the Central Line, and modifications to trains being sent to the Piccadilly to increase services there, meant that the Bakerloo was losing standard stock to Acton. The Bakerloo's own stock was replaced first by the cars stored at Neasden, then by those used on the Stanmore line and eventually by the transfer of three 4-car trains of 1938 stock to Neasden to work the Stanmore line in place of the Standard stock. When the Metropolitan/Bakerloo changeover took place on 1st October 1939, these three units became part of the Bakerloo fleet.

The inaugural trip to the reconstructed ex-LNER station at East Finchley, performed by a 1938 stock train in July 1939. LT Museum

The original shovel-type lampshade provided on 1938 stock. Note the part of the line diagram showing unopened sections of the Northern Line. LT Museum

On the Underground it had often been the practice to devise some sort of joint or part ownership of rolling stock running over lines owned by other companies. In the case of the Bakerloo Line to Watford, for example, two-thirds of the cars originally used to work the service were owned by the London & North Western Railway (whose line it was north of Queens Park) and, in the case of the District Line to Barking (and later Upminster), about 10% of the cars were owned by the London, Tilbury & Southend Railway (later the LMS). Such schemes were abandoned in the early 1930s by both the LMS and the GWR, the two railway companies which then had joint rolling stock agreements with the Underground. In other examples of joint operation, working expenses and revenue were shared, e.g. the Southern Railway lines to Richmond and Wimbledon, whilst the rolling stock was owned by the operator providing the service. For some reason not entirely clear, the LNER reverted to the old scheme of part ownership for the 1938 stock.

The scheme proposed was based on the idea that a proportion of the 1938 cars should be owned by the LNER, this proportion being based on the number of cars required to work the train services over the LNER owned portion of lines. In November 1937 this was calculated as follows:

Central   11 x 7, 8 x 8 and 6 x 2 cars (153 cars)
Northern   18 x 7 and 2 x 6 cars   (138 cars)

This idea was soon abandoned and a new scheme devised based, not on services but on mileage. The number of cars for each section then became:

Central: 136 Northern: 160

Eventually a final, adjusted mileage calculation was worked out and it was decided to allocate individual cars to the LNER. This was done in August 1939 as follows:

Central	Northern	Cars	Numbers
80	92	DM	10238-323/11239-323
17	24	NDM	12117-12157
32	44	T	012313-388
129 +	160	= 289	Total

Since individual cars had been allocated to the LNER, it was necessary to provide some form of ownership indication on the cars themselves. A plate was therefore fixed to one end of the solebar on each side of the car which read:

'PROPERTY OF THE LNER'

Some cars entered service before this was done but all cars were eventually so marked and many of them lasted until they were scrapped. Ownership by the LNER actually ceased in 1948 when the British Transport Commission was inaugurated and London Transport took over ownership of the cars.

In recognition of the line ownership by the LNER of parts of the Northern and Central Lines, a number of 1938 cars were the property of the LNER until Nationalisation in 1948. Many of these cars retained their specially fitted ownership plates until their withdrawal. The late P.W. Boulding

Chapter 2
Design

Despite the outbreak of war, deliveries of 1938 stock continued throughout 1940 and only ceased in early 1941 after they had gradually fallen from full production in October 1939 to a trickle of a few a month in August 1940. Deliveries actually ceased in June 1941 with 1094 cars delivered, a total of 1000 recorded as having entered service and 27 outstanding delivery. Deliveries were not to restart until 1946. This is perhaps the point at which to look at the design of the 1938 stock.

The biggest disadvantage of tube car design before 1935 was the fact that part of the potential passenger carrying capacity was lost to equipment. The design of the original tube trains built in 1903-6 was based on a power unit being provided at each end of a 6-car train. The power equipment was fitted on and over the outer end bogie immediately behind the driver's cab. To permit the installation of large enough traction motors on the bogie, the driving wheel diameter had to be increased from the tube trailer size of 31 inches to 36 inches and the floor height from 2 feet above rail level in the passenger saloon areas to 3ft 9ins. The raised floor area was thus lost to passengers because it reduced the internal height of the car to 5ft 3ins. Instead, it was used to house traction control equipment and the air compressor, neither of which would fit below the car floor.

All subsequent tube stock had been built to this design. By the time the standard tube stock was in mid-production in 1927, the original 6-car formation had been increased to 7 cars by the addition of a third driving motor car in the middle of the train. Of the 7 cars, three now had an equipment compartment causing each to have a loss of 33% of its passenger accommodation. This resulted in a 15% loss for the whole train. Elimination of this loss was regarded as an important objective.

What was wanted was a reduction in equipment size which would allow it all to go under the car floors. The actual space available was 17½ inches between the underframe members and the track clearances. To fit motors, compressors, traction control contractors and all the other bits and pieces needed for the train's operation in this small area was no mean achievement but it was done, and it allowed a 15% increase in passenger accommodation on a 7-car train.

Exactly how the train equipment was made to fit under the 1935 and 1938 stock floors we shall see later, but some careful body and frame design was necessary as well and it is interesting to see how the design evolved from earlier types.

The genesis of the 1935-8 structural design already existed in the trailer cars built in 1931 as part of the Standard stock order for the Piccadilly Line extensions. These were 40-seat cars with two double and two single sliding doorways on each side. The single doors were at the extreme ends of the car. The 1931 cars were the first to have them, as earlier cars of 1923-30 vintage had only the double doorways. The car body had to be extended to accommodate the extra single doors and, in order to keep within the gauge envelope, the body sides were slightly tapered inwards at their ends.

The same general layout was applied to the 1938 stock car body design without the clerestory roof common on earlier tube cars. The window area was increased and the seating layout was changed, although the number of seats remained at forty for trailer cars. For driving cars, which differed from trailers only in having a cab at one end in place of the single sliding doors, the seating was increased by two to forty-two.

The most complex part of the 1935-8 car design was in the layout of the underframe. Because of the low floor height of tube cars, it had always been necessary to design the underframe so that the wheels protruded into the underframe area. This area had to be left open and the seating was arranged so that longitudinal seats were positioned over the wheels and, with the main longitudes, which also acted as seat risers, formed a neat box over them. The same principle was applied to the 1938 stock but with the main longitudinal members raised slightly to allow the necessary clearance for the traction motors, which were mounted between the wheels.

The raised underframe design also involved a raised car floor (as mentioned earlier) but only by 4 inches and only between the longitudinal seats over the bogies. The rest of the floor was at the normal level. Gently sloping ramps were provided at either end of the raised areas but they were quite unobtrusive and probably went unnoticed by the majority of travellers. The same design was used on the 1959/62 stocks.

The raised floors were necessary to allow running clearances over the bogies. The traction motors were much smaller than previous designs and could be used to drive a 31-inch wheel but they were a tight fit. The bogie was also an unusual and very compact design and it was too tight a fit. All cars, whether having motors or not, had the same design of frame and bogie. Apart from the advantages of standardisation, it allowed additional motors to be added in the future if improved performance was wanted.

Although there were actually 10 different types of 1938 car there were only two body types. The remaining differences were in the equipment fitted, in particular the special arrangements made for the 9-car trains. The two main body designs were the driving car and the non-driving or trailer cars.

The general shape of the 1938 body was based originally on the 1931 trailer, as mentioned above, but the principles of underfloor traction equipment, small motors and new bogies and frames were first tried on the 1935 experimental cars. Of the 24 cars of this stock, the first 18 had the streamlined driving end. All the cars had cabs and they were formed in back-to-back pairs, three to a train, to make up 6-car trains. All cars were motor cars. There were no trailers, hence the need to order three extra trailers as part of the 1938 order to allow these trains to be made up to 7 cars.

The streamlined cabs, as Graff-Baker thought, were really only bowing to fashion. Streamlining was not effective below speeds of 80 mph and it used a lot of extra space. The central driving position and the special joystick controls were disliked by the drivers. In addition, the London Passenger Transport Board didn't like it either. As we have seen, there were doubts expressed about the aesthetics of two coupled streamlined ends and that was when Graff-Baker was asked to try the flat-ended design. This appeared on the fourth 6-car train of 1935 stock and this was really the final prototype for the 1938 stock design.

The 1938 body design was only a tidying-up of the flat-fronted 1935 design. The standard layout of body for both motor and trailer was adopted, the only difference between them being the provision of the driver's cab and two additional passenger seats at one end of the motor car. The design was to become so successful that it remained the standard for tube cars for almost 30 years and was only superseded in production by the 1967 tube stock.

Equipment

The primary rolling stock design objective of recovering the passenger space lost to equipment was thus finally achieved with the prototype 1935 tube stock and went into production with the 1938 stock. The compression of the equipment to fit below a 2ft high car floor was a significant step forward and was probably the biggest single advance made in rolling stock equipment design until the introduction of automatically driven trains on the Victoria Line in 1968.

The revolutionary aspects of the 1938 stock equipment design can be divided into three main areas: traction equipment, auxiliary equipment and pneumatic equipment. All had to be reduced in size to fit

under the car floors and, in addition, there had to be careful arrangement of the equipment to make it accessible for maintenance.

The most significant advances in equipment design were those involving traction control equipment. Several different systems were offered to the LPTB by different manufacturers and they were tried out on various cars of the 1935 experimental stock. General Electric, Metropolitan Vickers, Allen West-Crompton Parkinson and British Thomson-Houston all offered systems, Allen West and GEC both offering two different schemes. In the end, the BTH system was the one accepted for use on the 1938 stock and it has been the basis upon which almost all subsequent Underground traction control systems have been based.

The various types of traction equipment on the 1935 experimental units were originally to have been arranged as follows:

10000-11000	Allen West/Crompton Parkinson multi-notch faceplate control with double glazing and 'air-conditioning'.
10001-11001	As above, with air conditioning.
10002-11002	Allen/West Crompton Parkinson straight multi-notch camshaft system.
10003-11003	GEC motor-driven camshaft control.
10004-11004	GEC motor-driven camshaft control.
10005-11005	GEC motor-driven camshaft control.
10006-11006	PCM control by BTH
10007-11007	PCM control by BTH
10008-11008	PCM control by BTH
10009-11009	MV oil-operated power drum system.
10010-11010	MV oil-operated power drum system.
10011-11011	MV oil-operated power drum system.

However, before all the units were completed, there was a shuffling around of some cars and equipment. Units 10003-11003 and 10006-11006 exchanged numbers in March 1936 before delivery, and the equipment finished up as follows:

10000-11000	Allen West/Crompton Parkinson multi-notch faceplate control with double glazing. Car 10000 was fitted with air conditioning by J. Stone, and 11000 by R. Crittall.
10001-11001	Allen West/Crompton Parkinson straight faceplate control. No air-conditioning.
10002-11002	GEC multi-notch camshaft system.
10003-11003	PCM control by BTH.
10004-11004	GEC staggered multi-notch camshaft control system.
10005-11005	Allen West/Crompton Parkinson straight camshaft system.
10006-11006	GEC staggered multi-notch camshaft control system.
10007-11007	PCM control by BTH.
10008-11008	PCM control by BTH.
10009-11009	MV oil-operated power drum system.
10010-11010	MV oil-operated power drum system.
10011-11011	MV oil-operated power drum system.

One of the 18 streamlined 1935 experimental cars being converted to a trailer in Acton Works, showing the new car end framing at the original driving end. The passenger emergency handle and its connecting pipework can be seen fitted in position. Note the slope of the car floor necessary to clear the bogie. LT Museum

ALLEN WEST/CROMPTON PARKINSON had three schemes:

1. Unit 10000-11000 had a series-parallel arrangement using two faceplate controllers, one for each motor circuit cutting out the starting resistances, both faceplates being driven by a 50-volt pilot motor. Each faceplate had 25 segments bridged by the arm which moved in a circle round the segments. The arm made one revolution each for series, parallel and weak-field providing 57 notches for the complete sequence. In addition to the faceplate there was an electro-pneumatically operated camshaft contactor unit which made the necessary power circuit changes from series to parallel. There were interlocks in the camshaft and the contactor group to ensure that the right sequence of switching was maintained. A double-pole line breaker to isolate the equipment in the 'off' position was also provided.

2 Unit 10001-11001: In this equipment, the two motors were in permanent parallel. The faceplate was also used to cut out resistance but because there was no switching from series to parallel, only one faceplate was required, and the interlocking was simplified. The theory at this time was that with increased acceleration the saving in current by series-parallel connection would be offset by the simplification in the switching. (A similar arrangement was suggested for the Tyne & Wear Metro, and has been incorporated on their stock.)

3. Unit 10005-11005: A motor-driven camshaft took the place of the two faceplates for cutting out resistance on a series-parallel combination of the traction motors.

The GENERAL ELECTRIC COMPANY (10002/4/6-11002/4/6) also employed a camshaft driven by a series motor energised at 50-volts for series-parallel and weak field connections. The camshaft made three revolutions from 'off' to full 'weak field', a total of 56 notches. Electro-pneumatic contactors were used to provide line switching and transition. One of the GEC units was arranged to have the motors in permanent parallel with a simplification in switching and a re-arrangement of the resistance steps. One feature of the GEC camshaft was that it was based on time with only an overriding current control if it rose to an excessive value, so that the notching was at virtually a constant rate irrespective of the train loading.

The BRITISH THOMSON-HOUSTON scheme (10003/7/8-11003/7/8) was the only one which was based on equipment which had operating experience, since the system was already in use on some trains in New York; not with identical equipment but similar and working to the same principles. The main difference with the experimental PCM units compared with the production version was that each piece of switch gear was mounted separately on the underframe, sometimes with its own cover, whereas the subsequent 1938 tube stock equipment was all mounted in an equipment box and designed with this in mind. Thus, sizes and fixing arrangements were different, otherwise the method of operation was the same.

The METROPOLITAN VICKERS scheme (10009/10/11-11009/10/11) used an oil-driven power drum for operating all resistance switching with a total of 45 notches. This switching was a combination of cutting out series and parallel steps of the resistance banks, and to avoid sparking one notch was always in contact. A large number of values were thereby obtained but the heating of the resistance was spread over the whole bank fairly evenly. The drum was driven round slowly and had to be stepped accurately under the control of the current. This equipment gave considerable trouble in spite of these points. Often, the contacts fused and the drum insulation failed. There were, in addition, six electro-pneumatic unit switches and an electro-pneumatic reverser.

Metropolitan Vickers equipped unit 10009-11009. LT Museum

1938 stock in the overhaul works at Acton. Driving motor car 11217 is on high in the lifting shop with a 1931 Standard stock trailer behind it. The 1938 stock body design was a development of the 1931 stock design with altered doorway positions and a new non-clerestory roof. LT Museum

The traction motors for the experimental trains were all made by Crompton Parkinson and were of type C200. Here again, the approach was made by Graff-Baker's team to motor manufacturers for a traction motor to go under a tube car. The existing manufacturers, GEC and MV, would not deviate from their standard designs without considerable encouragement and Graff-Baker found a more helpful attitude at Cromptons, who wanted to regain their traction know-how.

The C200 motor was designed with a long armature and compact case so that the floor of the tube car had to be raised only a few inches to accommodate it. Subsequently, of course, the traditional makers squealed when they thought that Cromptons were going to get an extremely large exclusive order for traction motors; although it would probably have been impossible for Cromptons to achieve the delivery requirements. Thus the idea was that the design would be owned by Lon-

don Transport, Cromptons being paid for their design work, but the motor could then be made to LT specification by any motor manufacturer. GEC therefore constructed a large number of the LT100 motor, which was a development of the C200, for use on the 1938 stock.

The traditional equipment manufacturers produced only one design each for all the cars of their respective trains and these were developments of equipment which already existed to a large extent in the case of BTH, and to a minor extent in the case of MV and GEC out of the whole deal for new traction equipment eventually settled upon for new tube and surface stock during the 1936-40 period, BTH received the contract for the tube traction equipment, GEC and Cromptons the contract for tube motors, and MV the contract for the traction equipment for the surface stock – their famous Metadyne system – and shared the motors contract with GEC. In the end, therefore, everyone was happy.

The Pneumatic Camshaft Mechanism (PCM) consisted of a number of air-operated units controlled by magnet valves. By a unique arrangement of motor and resistance circuits, the camshaft controller was arranged to cut out resistance during series acceleration by rotating in one direction, and after transition from series to parallel reversed its direction to cut out the resistance again in returning to its 'off' position.

The camshaft controller was driven by a pneumatic engine consisting of two cylinders, the pistons of which were connected together by a rack. Oil under pressure was used to drive the camshaft forward, and air pressure used to return it to the 'off' position. The camshaft was allowed to advance in a series of steps by a star-shaped wheel mounted on its end. An electrically controlled arm locked the starwheel when the camshaft was in the correct position and, when required, the arm was released thus allowing the camshaft to advance to the next position. This could be used by the driver when desired to stop the progress of notching up. He could, with some deft movements of the controller handle, notch up by hand.

A series-parallel transfer switch was provided, consisting of an electro-pneumatic switch with a single air cylinder operating three contactors through cam surfaces; one contactor was normally open, and the other two normally closed. The operation of three contacts by a single unit ensured a quick positive transition without the need for electrical interlocking. The following running characteristics were available:

– Inch or shunt:
Full field with motors in series and all resistance cut in to provide very slow speed.
– Series:
Full field with all resistance cut out to provide medium speed.
– Parallel:
Full field with all resistance cut out to provide normal full speed.
– Weak Field:
As parallel but with extra resistance in the field circuit to increase speed further.

The master controller was of the upright, geared pattern and had a reverse drum with four positions, one 'reverse', one 'off' and two 'forward' positions controlled by the operation of the driver's reverser key. 'Forward 1' gave a low rate of acceleration suitable for open running on wet rail while 'Forward 2' gave a higher rate of acceleration meant for tunnel or dry rail operation. The 'off' position locked the main drum and handle and allowed the deadman's handle to be released. The reverse position gave the lower rate of acceleration.

Tappings were provided on the field shunting resistances giving 75%, 70%, 65% and 60% motor field strength and field shunting was taken in two steps. No weak field notch was provided on the master controller but a weak field switch was incorporated in the marker light unit. This switch, when closed, showed a black and yellow striped metal flag behind the cab window over the marker light unit (indicating to an outside observer whether the shunted field feature was in use or not) and energised the field shunting train wire.

Acceleration was automatic, the camshaft controller notching up to the required position under the control of an accelerating relay. With the weak field switch closed and after full parallel had been reached, the intermediate weak field notch was taken under the control of the accelerating relay, the final weak field stage being under the control of a field shunt relay. All the traction control circuits were operated from a 50-volt supply obtained from the motor generator set, of which more later.

Two line breakers were provided which were operated directly from the Master Controller by means of magnet valves. These carried out all main current breaking, the cam operated resistance switches on the camshaft controller never being called upon to break under load. An overload relay was fitted with trip and reset coils and controlled by push buttons from the driver's cab. A standard type current relay with two series coils (one in each motor circuit) was provided so that the notching current in parallel was the mean of the two motor currents.

It is interesting to note that an early version of the PCM scheme may have been tried on the Underground during the mid-1920s. A description of a 'Pneumatic Camshaft Control' system, using 600-volt control circuits (instead of the 50-volts of the 1938 PCM system) and a purely air-operated camshaft without oil damping, appeared in a 1927 publication 'Electric Trains' by R.E. Dickenson. A full description, with diagrams, is given, together with the statement that it was fitted to the 'later stock' of the London Electric Railway. Obviously Dickenson, who wrote the book in Australia, was referring to the 1927 Standard tube stock, which had BTH equipment, but it was of their electro-magnetic design, not the pneumatic camshaft control system. However, it is not unreasonable to assume that BTH would try to sell their new system to such a large customer as the London Underground and it seems possible that a trial equipment was fitted to a tube car about 1925, which may thus have prompted Dickenson's statement.

The biggest obstacle to size reduction of traction control equipment had been the provision of suitable power circuit switches, called contactors. Power control systems as used on London Underground cars at the time, called for any of the fourteen contactors in the motor circuit to be able to be opened whilst carrying maximum motor current. To do this they had to be large, heavy duty switches, each with its own operating mechanism and arc blow-out system. The beauty of the new BTH equipment was that the number of these contactors was reduced to two (the Line Breakers) and their design was compact enough to fit under a tube car floor.

The elimination of the bulk of the heavy duty contactors was achieved by mounting all the power circuit switches so that they were opened or closed by the common camshaft. Their individual control and interlocking systems were eliminated. The use of the camshaft which was driven by an air operated, oil-damped, rack and pinion system, eventually gave rise to the title Pneumatic Camshaft Mechanism, which was the British identification for the system.

Another feature which considerably reduced the size of the PCM equipment was the use of the same contactors for parallel and series running. By use of a clever circuit configuration, the cam operated contactors were actuated in the series sequence while the camshaft rotated in one direction and then in the parallel sequence while the camshaft rotated in the opposite direction. In fact, the camshaft was in the same position while the train was running in the full parallel position as when the equipment was in the off position. This saved a great deal of unnecessary 'running back' of the camshaft. Operating time was saved and mechanical wear was reduced. It was a very neat system.

Motors and Motor Generators

The traditional tube car traction motor was rated at 240hp and it drove a 36 inch wheel. Its design changed little between 1914 and 1934 and only with the introduction of the 1935 experimental stock was there any significant advance. Now the motor was rated at 168hp and was small enough to drive a 31-inch wheel.

Of course, the drop from the old 240hp motor to 168hp caused a relocation of the motors on the train. On the Standard tube stock, three motor cars each carried 2 x 240hp motors on the leading bogie. This gave a total of 1440hp per train. For the 1938 tube stock the number of motor cars was increased to five each with two motors, which gave a total of 1680hp per train.

An innovation on the 1938 stock was the provision of a 50-volt DC auxiliary current system, first tried on the 1935 stock and also used on the 1937-8 built O and P stocks on the surface lines of the Underground. Hitherto, most trains used the line voltage of 630 volts for all auxiliary equipment as well as the power circuits but, for the new trains, 50 volts was adopted. This subsequently became the standard control voltage on LT railways.

The use of a 50-volt DC auxiliary system allowed control circuits to be separated completely from the power circuits, allowed lighter components and wiring to be used, allowed elimination of special control resistors and allowed an earth or chassis return to be adopted. The motor-generator-battery system used also eliminated the complex battery charging needed on Standard tube stock and it simplified the lighting system.

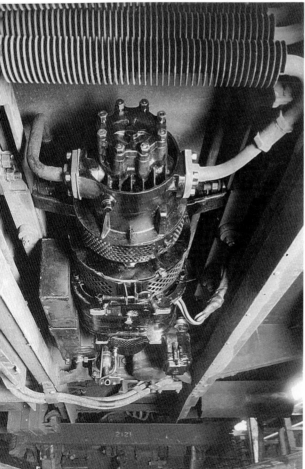

Top **The underside of a 'D' driving motor car lifted off its bogies. On the left, immediately next to the two curved air hoses, is the five-valve auto-coupler disconnecting unit.** LT Museum

Left **This is the Achilles' heel of the 1938 tube stock, the KLL4 rotary compressor. Designed to fit in the confined space under trams and trolleybuses and seen here in position between the longitudes of a 1938 stock non-driving motor car, it did not stand the rigours of Underground service well and was a constant source of trouble until it was replaced by newer types of compressor during the 1970s.** LT Museum

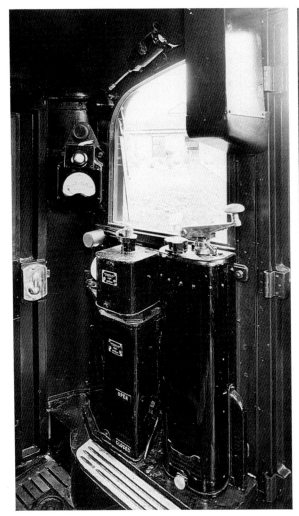

Above Left **The driving cab of the 1938 stock in original condition. To the left of the windscreen is the speedometer. Above it is the MG indicator light and above that the sequence light, which showed when all motors were working in parallel. Both the sequence lights and speedo's were allowed to become disused over the years because of their unreliability.** LT Museum

Above Right **The right hand guard's door control panel of 1938 stock in original condition. It has the flaps over the open buttons to prevent inadvertent operation and lacks the passenger open light provided after the Second World War. The pilot light, originally mounted in the ceiling, was repositioned on the control panels on all EHO trains.** LT Museum

The provision of the 50-volt supply was arranged so that a small 600 volt motor drove a 50v DC generator all the time the train was in service. A battery floated across the generator terminals was available to supply 50 volts if the generator stopped – as it would over current rail gaps – and it used the generator output to keep it charged. It was arranged so that the generator, located on the driving motor cars, would supply the main lighting for that car and, if necessary, the adjacent car. The battery did not supply main lighting, only 4 emergency bulbs on each car.

The type 33 motor generators built by Met Vickers and provided for the 1938 stock, and also the surface O and P stocks, were fitted with fans to keep the machines cool. The noise from these fans gave the stock a distinctive 'blowing' sound which is well remembered by those who were familiar with them. The absence of this reassuring sound is also remembered by those, like the author, who drove the stock and who had cause to miss it when the machine failed on them. The action required then was to get back to depot using only the battery in the hope that it would last long enough.

As with the traction and braking systems, a complete redesign of the old London Electric Railway Standard stock auxiliary systems had taken place and had been tried out on the 1935 cars prior to its inclusion in the 1938 design.

Some interesting design problems arose out of this work, in particular because of the very restricted space available under the cars. The most well-known concerned the air compressor. Traditional designs used on all Underground lines had been large reciprocating, duplex pumps, driven at relatively slow speed through reduction gears. They were usually reliable, particularly the BTH types, and of them some lasted for over 70 years, working under various different stocks.

Their chief drawback was that they were too large to fit under a tube car floor. They had always been located in the switch compartment behind the driver's cab with the traction equipment and, when the under-floor traction equipment design for the 1935 stock arrived, a new, smaller compressor had to be found.

The compressors provided for the 1935 stock were of two types, both based on designs used on tramcars and trolleybuses. One type was the Electro-Mechanical Brake Company's 36H4 machine, a four-cylinder reciprocating pump, which was fitted to five units, and the other was the KLL4 rotary compressor made by Bernard Holland Engineering under licence from the Swiss Locomotive Machine Works (SLM). The KLL4 was chosen for the main order of 1938 tube stock and the 'P' class surface stock. Its precision design, coming as it did with the watchmaking tolerances imposed by the Swiss engineers, proved very vulnerable to the rigours of London Underground service. It was quickly affected by dirt, vibration and lubrication failures, and by 'make-do-and-mend' maintenance during the Second World War. By the early 1970s all had been replaced by modern reciprocating compressors.

The KLL4 design was unusual, for the Underground at least, in that it was a rotary pump which compressed air by using vanes mounted eccentrically about a drive shaft. It ran at a much faster rate than a reciprocating pump and apart from being smaller, it was also much quieter. It was so quiet in fact that it was difficult to tell the difference between the sound it made and that of a motor generator, unless you were 'in the know'.

As with a Standard stock train, three compressors per 7-car train were provided on 1938 stock. One was fitted under each of the two trailers and the other under the NDM. Even the '58 trailers' also each had one. For the first time on a tube train, a synchronised control system was adopted. As soon as the air pressure on one car dropped low enough to cause the compressor to start, all the other compressors on the train started as well. This was intended to give a faster build up of pressure but it was largely negated by the smaller than usual capacity of the pumps which, although they were nominally rated at 30cu ft/min, rarely achieved it.

As with any radical departure from standard design, the new compressors gave much trouble during their early years. However, unlike most innovative systems which often go through a shakedown period before settling down, the KLL4s never really worked satisfactorily.

One problem which came to light very early on was the control system. The synchronising circuits had been arranged to switch off automatically when the driver took out his control key. This meant that if a train was left unattended for any more than a few minutes the main reservoir air pressure would begin to leak away and would not be replaced. When a driver came to start a train therefore, he had to wait while it 'pumped up' before he could release the brakes. Those who remember how long it took to 'open up' a 38 in more recent times when it had more modern compressors, will no doubt sympathise with drivers who had this problem in the 'all KLL4' days. A modification was quickly put in to ensure that the compressors could run without a control switch being closed. Now they could maintain the main reservoir air pressure on an unattended train.

Other problems which soon appeared involved the bearings, which often failed, the oil pumps, the vanes and damage to the externally mounted pipework which was rather exposed and, even if it survived a few weeks in service, often got damaged when the pump was removed from under the car during maintenance. Naturally, the onset of the War did not help the problems because of shortages of labour and materials at home and because some of the parts were made in Germany and spares were unobtainable.

Even taking into account the war, it was eventually realised that the KLL4s were never going to be reliable and when the post-war rearrangement of the 38s was carried out during the 1949 Uncoupling Programme and some extra compressors were required, they were of a new type, the Westinghouse DHC2. This reverted to a reciprocating pump design but it was now small enough to fit under a tube car floor. It was supplied for the 1949 cars and the R surface stock also built at this time. It too had its troubles in the early days but at least it settled down to a reasonably uneventful if not quite existence (it was much noisier than the KLL4).

Eventually all the KLL4s were replaced. In fact, most of them were scrapped before the cars they had supplied. During the first scrapping programme of the stock in the early 1970s, all the KLL4s were disposed of and the cars which remained were fitted with DHC2s, DHC5As (a later version of the DHC2) and the Reavell TBC38Z, a similar type supplied for the A60 surface stock.

The demise of the KLL4s was in part due to a strike. Between September and December 1969 there was a three-month stoppage of work at Acton Works due to a dispute. At that time the operation of 1938 stock depended on a constant flow of repaired KLL4 compressors from the works to replace those which had failed. As soon as the flow stopped, the train service on the Northern and Bakerloo Lines began to suffer. There were wholesale cancellations on both lines and this episode can now clearly be seen as the beginning of the end for the 1938 stock. More on this later.

Brakes

The innovatory theme playing throughout the 1938 traction and auxiliary equipment designs was continued for the pneumatic equipment, particularly train braking. Some new features were also included in the door equipment but these had almost all appeared on other stocks in some form or another and were only refined for the 1938 stock.

The braking system provided on both the 1935 and 1938 stocks was called the self-lapping electro-pneumatic brake. It was another product of the extraordinary combination of the inventiveness of Graff-Baker's design team at Acton and his persuasiveness in getting manufacturers to co-operate in design work, in this case the Westinghouse Brake & Signal Co, then based at King's Cross.

Over the ten years before the introduction of the 1938 stock, there had been some significant improvements in train braking systems on the Underground. The traditional Westinghouse supplied system – known as the quick-acting pneumatic brake – was being superseded by electrically controlled systems. The advantages were clear: rapid application and release, simultaneous operation throughout the train, less mechanical wear and tear and more precise stopping at stations.

The old pneumatic system worked by means of changes in air pressure in a pipe (the brake pipe, called the train line in London) which, when pressurised with compressed air, allowed the brakes on the train to release and, when exhausted, caused the brakes to apply. The pipe was only used as a control medium. The brake blocks were applied to the wheel tread by air pressure in a brake cylinder. The air entered the cylinder from a storage reservoir (called the auxiliary reservoir) through a controlling valve (the triple valve) and was exhausted from the cylinder again through the triple valve. With the pipe charged, the triple valve let any air in the brake cylinders escape and the brakes were released. At the same time, the auxiliary reservoir was recharged (from the brake pipe) ready for another brake application.

If the air from the brake pipe escaped, the triple valve detected it. It plugged the release port and let air from the auxiliary reservoir enter the brake cylinders. The brakes went on. The degree of application depended on the level of loss in the brake pipe. The driver let air out of the brake pipe in little 'blows' through his brake valve in the cab. His first blow got the blocks on the wheels. He would then estimate how rapidly the train was decelerating and 'give it another

The 1938 tube stock had, for the first time, individual brake cylinders for each block. This is a double set, complete with handbrake linkage. The flanged cast iron block weighed over 30 lbs. Modern composition blocks weigh about 8 lbs. LT Museum

blow' if he needed more to get the train to stop in the right place. His job was complicated by the fact that the changes in brake pipe pressure took time to reach all the cars on the trains so not all cars initially braked at the same time.

Naturally, this system required a certain level of skill. The nature of the system was such that it was possible to get graduated applications (using a 'blow' every so often) but not a graduated release. Because of this, if the driver put too much brake on, he had to release it, recharge the auxiliary reservoirs and then reapply. Even if he overcame the danger of misjudging the release and leaving the reapplication too late, causing an overrun, time was lost releasing and reapplying.

Its real advantage was that it was safe. If anything went wrong, the brake applied. Loss of air in the brake pipe caused the brakes to go on, regardless of the cause. An uncoupled train, broken pipe, burst hose, passenger emergency handle or deadman valve operation could all cause a brake application. It was not gradual like the one initiated by the driver's brake valve but sudden and up to maximum limits available.

For almost the whole of the existence of electric traction from the late 1890s, a means of improving brake control (whilst still retaining the fail-safe feat-ures) had been sought. At first in the United States before World War I and then during the same war in Britain, various schemes for electrical control of braking had been tried with varying degrees of success. Eventually, in 1928, the District Railway introduced an electrically controlled braking system which allowed the flexibility of air brakes, the speed of electrical response and the safety of the Westinghouse brake. By the time the 1938 stock was introduced, it had reached the pinnacle of its development in the self-lapping form and become standard equipment on the Underground until the early 1960s.

The principle of the e.p. brake was that the brake pipe was not used for control. It remained charged and so did the auxiliary reservoir. The triple valve was in the 'brake-release' position, and the electrical control was superimposed on it by providing an application valve and a holding valve on each car. The holding valve let air into the brake cylinder. Instead of using air from the auxiliary reservoir, air from the main reservoir was used. The valves were controlled by train wires connected to the driver's brake valve, which had a couple of extra positions added to it.

Now the driver had instant air braking on every car. He had an inexhaustible air supply fed into the main reservoir directly to the brake unit on each car. He had

One of the problems encountered by 1938 stock when it was first delivered was the brake cylinder size. Testing of brakes and types of blocks was delayed by long sunny spells and dry weather. After the Second World War a water spray was installed over the fast line between Acton Town and South Ealing to allow wet rail testing without waiting for the right weather. A 1938 stock train is seen here on test just after the installation of the sprays in 1946. Everything else in the scene seems wet too! LT Museum

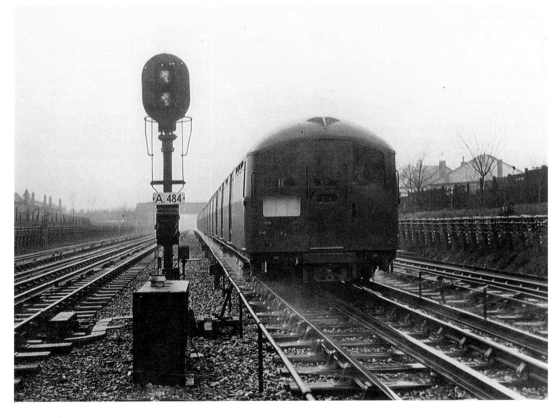

graduated release by opening the holding valves whenever he wanted to and he could now, as they used to say in those days, 'stop his train on a sixpence'.

The self-lapping feature was a control refinement which allowed the driver to vary the rate of braking by positioning his brake valve handle between 'off' and 'full application'. Older e.p. fitted trains had separate 'off', 'holding' and 'application' positions which required the driver to reach the desired braking rate by moving his handle to 'application' until that rate was reached and then select 'holding'.

Another refinement was the mercury retardation controller or retarder as it was commonly called. This was a pair of longitudinally mounted, mercury filled circular glass tubes which detected the rate of deceleration by virtue of the mercury moving inside and shorting out electrical contacts mounted at various points along the tube. This prevented any brake application beyond a predetermined limit. If the limit was exceeded, which was naturally inclined to occur at lower speeds, the mercury moved further up the tube, shorting out more contacts which caused the retarder to blow excess air out of the brake cylinders through a 'blow-down valve. The retarders thus acted as switches which controlled first the application valve and then the blow-down valve on each car.

The system was introduced to reduce the level of flatted wheels, which had become very high on e.p. fitted trains. The early e.p. trains had cast iron blocks and they gave a high rate of braking at the lower end of the speed range which often caused skidding. The introduction of retarders (and the use of non-metallic brake blocks in later years) helped to reduce the incidence of flatted wheels.

Doors

As was by then standard on all new Underground trains, the 1938 tube stock was fitted with air-worked doors under overall control of the guard located on the last car. They were also fitted with passenger door control. Strangely though, the 1935 experimental cars did not have passenger door control, although it had been introduced on a couple of trains on the Hammersmith and City Line in 1935. It may have had something to do with the fact that the 1935 stock was intended for the Piccadilly Line and this was the only

tube line never to have had passenger door control.

Passenger door control was introduced to allow train doors to be kept closed unless required to open for boarding or alighting passengers. As originally used, it was arranged so that the guard operated a 'passenger open' button at his control position to release the 'push-to-open' buttons provided at each doorway. Passengers then opened the doors at the doorway they wished to use. If required, the guard could open all the doors by means of a 'normal open' button. The advantage of this system over the original system where all doors always opened was the ability to reduce the heat loss from inside the cars during cold weather. It was a good selling point for the long runs in the open.

Like many good ideas which looked wonderful in theory, continued to look good on the drawing board and still worked when put on trial, this one soon ran into serious trouble when it went into service on a large scale. Very soon, passengers began to complain of being carried past their stop because the doors didn't open. Of course, in the majority of cases it was because the passenger had not operated the button. They had not got used to the system. They were further confused because passenger open was only used in open sections, not at tunnel stations. At tunnel stations the guard opened all the doors.

There were, however, more serious difficulties. A number of technical problems arose, particularly because of the use of only one button to open doors. Doors did sometimes get opened in error as guards were used to having to press two buttons to open doors. Some circuit anomalies also came to light with the discovery of a number of false door openings due to earthing of the open wire, short circuits and misuse of the controls by crews. Eventually, because of these problems, the passenger open system was withdrawn from all lines in January 1939.

Attempts to get a workable system continued however, and in February 1940, a train entered service on the Northern Line with modified equipment. Apart from safer circuitry, it was arranged so that the guard had to open his own door before opening the passenger doors or switching in 'passenger open'. The train ran for a short time but was withdrawn pending the end of the war because it was decided not to continue with 'passenger open' in wartime.

A 1938 stock train with a '58' trailer at South Kenton in May 1950. J.E. Cull

Soon after the 1938 stock began entering service another serious problem began to appear. There were several incidents of doors opening whilst the train was running. Many of the cases involved the '58' trailers. At the time, late in 1938, almost all the conversion work on the '58' trailers had been completed and by mid-November 21 of them were in service on the Northern Line. In fact, all but 6 of them were programmed to enter service on the Bakerloo but work on them had proceeded more quickly than delivery of new cars to run with them. Eventually the car builders were asked to hold back construction of trailers so that the '58' trailers could go into service. Graff-Baker was anxious not to let them deteriorate in storage and he was also very short of siding space, so they were put into trains on the Northern as they were completed.

The door opening problem caused near panic amongst the management. That the doors only opened on '58' trailers pointed to a fault originating at Acton, either in design or during conversion. The car builders could not be blamed for it. Graff-Baker threatened to withdraw them all from service. A quick check was done to see how many were in service and how many new trailers could be used in their place. At that time there were three locations where new trailers were being prepared for service:

Cockfosters	7 cars
Ealing Common	10 cars
Golders Green	2 cars

The use of Cockfosters is interesting, but since it had a lot of spare undercover accommodation and Golders Green was rather cramped, it was a reasonable choice.

The 21 of the 58 trailers already in service at the end of November 1938 were the subject of many concentrated minds. A technical assistant was assigned to ride on one of the offending cars whilst it ran in service. He was provided with ammeters connected to the door valve open wires and spent some hours riding up and down the Northern Line watching the meters obediently register the doors opening at each station but never at any other time until . . . it happened. The doors opened between stations. However, the ammeters never registered. The doors opened but the wires were apparently not energised.

The train went to Morden, minus passengers, and was descended upon by the 'brass' from Acton. Much testing and discussion took place but no solution could be found. By now it was late in the day and frustration was beginning to set in. A solution had to be found. People could be killed if doors suddenly flew open in tunnels. One of the group huddled around an exposed door valve stood over it silently pondering. Suddenly, in a fit of pique he kicked at it and cursed. At that instant the doors flew open. Everyone was agog. Slowly they all began to realise what had happened. The kick had jolted the valve, lifted it and caused the doors to open. They now had the answer. Vibration was the cause. The valves had been mounted on an angled bracket which vibrated as the car ran. Any sharp jolt would cause the valve to lift and open the doors. The cars were all hurriedly withdrawn from service one Friday night and had stiffer brackets fitted over the weekend. Most of them were back in service on the following Monday morning.

Bogies

Another entirely new feature of the 1935 and 1938 stocks was the bogie design. Standard tube cars had used riveted, plate form bogies of fairly unremarkable but very reliable design suitably modified for the restricted space under a tube car. With riveted bogies though, there was a lot of maintenance work involved in replacing rivets which had worked loose. To overcome this problem, Graff-Baker proposed an all-

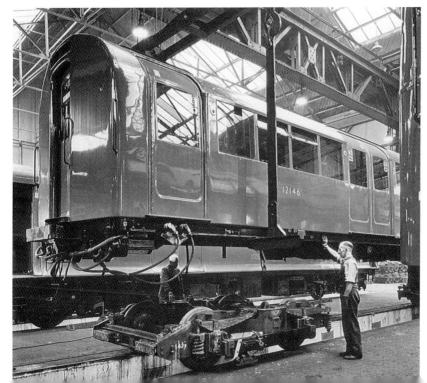

Acton Works in January 1953 showing a 1938 tube stock non-driving motor car being lowered onto its bogies after overhaul. LT Museum

45

welded bogie. It was also, as described earlier, to have a wide bolster suspension spacing to try to improve the ride. To accommodate this, the side frames were shaped with a bay on top of which the body side bearers were located.

This was another feature of the stock which was soon in trouble. Cracks began to appear in the frames and patches had to be installed. These tended to cause stresses to appear in other parts of the frame and more patches were added. Afterwards the whole bogie frame had to be heat treated to de-stress it. The work was done at Acton in a large oven capable of taking a whole frame.

The '58' trailers retained their original London Electric Railway type V2 bogies. These were of the traditional design and retained their foundation brake rigging operated by a single brake cylinder mounted on the car underframe. For the 1935-38 cars, this arrangement had been eliminated in favour of individual brake cylinders for each brake block – a total of 16 per car. This seemingly expensive arrangement was actually better than having a single cylinder for a number of reasons. The single cylinder was connected to each brake block by a multitude of rods and levers which needed very careful setting up to ensure an even application on each wheel. On many occasions flatted wheels were caused by maladjusted rigging and the uneven wear on brakes meant that rigging had to be readjusted every three days. To add to these problems, the wear on the links and pins was considerable and extensive bushing was necessary. Keeping all this ironwork in good condition was a full time job and a thriving cottage industry was employed at Acton on just this work.

The new brake cylinders were therefore regarded as a big improvement. A cylinder, or a pair of them if the inside-mounted blocks were involved, could be changed if necessary without disturbing the other cylinders. They could be individually adjusted and needed less attention as they were individually wear-compensating. Of course there was a snag. All the cylinders were connected to the brake unit containing the valves by a maze of pipes. These were jig-built and welded as a unit on the truck. There were soon breakages. The lack of flexibility in the pipework caused fractures and eventually flexible hoses were placed at vulnerable points to ease the stress. Another problem concerned the motor trucks. The space was so crowded near the motors, that changing brake blocks on the motored wheels was always difficult. It remained so to the end of the stock.

Special Features of 1935 Stock Equipment

The 1935 cars were provided with a number of interesting features which did not appear on the 1938 production cars. The driving position of the streamlined cars was in the centre of the cab with the connecting doorway immediately in front of the driver. This door on some cars was mounted on rail at the top and bottom to allow it to slide back and provide a through passage. On other cars the door was pivoted on to an enormous cast hinge which itself was pivoted to the car body below the nearside cab window. The central arm-chair-type driving seat had joystick driving controls with the brake stick on the left and the controller stick – complete with deadman push-button – on the right. The brake was – as on the 1938 stock – electro-pneumatic with mercury retardation control and self-lapping equipment. The Westinghouse air brake was retained for emergency use with a separate brake handle provided for the driver, next to the e.p. joystick.

The driving position made the driver's lookout very poor near the front of the train so, to allow easy coupling, a push-button for slow forward movement (usually called 'inching') was provided in a box mounted in the roof over the offside front window. A second button gave 'inching reverse'. An 'inching reverse' button was also provided on the nearside guard's panel. Operation of this allowed forward movement from the rear of the train with side lookout facilities – important for depot shunting movements.

An unusual feature of the guard's controls was the provision of only one 'open' button. On all trains built before and since, two open buttons were provided to give some protection against inadvertent opening. On the 1935 stock cars, protection was in the form of a hinged flap over the single button which had to be lifted while the button was pressed.

The 'air-conditioning' fitted to unit 10000-11000 was not really air-conditioning in its true sense. It was a forced ventilation system, which was heated in winter. Unfortunately, in the early days of operation, not only did the thermostat fail but so did the forced ventilation, on one occasion nearly asphyxiating the passengers. After this, it was never used again. It is not known when the car windows were converted to standard.

On all cars at the driving ends, automatic Wedglock couplers were provided, as were roller destination blinds and five square-shaped headlights. Coupling between cars of a unit was of the semi-permanent bar type. The compressor was fitted to the 10xxx cars and the motor generator to the 11xxx cars. It was possible for all types of experimental tube stock to be coupled together, but for passenger service the flat-fronted units always worked together.

On all 24 cars, the guard and his controls were located in the driving cabs, hence the cab doors were extended up into the curve of the roof, and hinged at the front, to allow access to the door controls on the rear wall, whereas 1938 tube stock cab doors were hinged at the back. The roller destination blinds were of the same material and style as used on LPTB buses; i.e. white lettering, black background.

The flat-ended train was much like the 1938 stock. The driver was on the traditional left-hand side of the cab and the end door was hinged. The handbrake was a lever, instead of a wheel as provided on the streamlined cars, and the seat was the tip-up type, long familiar on the District Line and subsequently LT standard. The drivers much preferred this train to the streamlined, armchair version.

On all 24 experimental cars, the master controller had five positions: the usual 'inch', 'series', and 'parallel', which are standard on all trains, plus two 'weakfield' positions.

Chapter 3
The War Years

The smooth progress of the New Works Programme was interrupted on 3rd September 1939 by the declaration of war between Britain and Germany. Up to this time, delivery of 1938 tube stock had continued fairly steadily and, pending some firm decisions on what action the government would take to divert manufacturing and labour efforts to wartime pursuits, it was to continue for some time. Expecting some changes in their programme, the LPTB did a review of work completed and outstanding as at 3rd September 1939. The position as regards 1938 stock was as follows:

Cars Delivered:566
Under Construction:101
Not yet started:454

The declaration of war did not prevent the introduction of the new Bakerloo services on 20th November 1939. The changeover of the Metropolitan's Stanmore line and local tracks to tube train working and all-day running through to Stanmore involved a complex series of stock changeovers. Some civil engineering finishing work was uncompleted and there were the usual teething troubles encountered with any new system.

The final version of the New Works Programme had intended that the Bakerloo would be worked by 34 x 7-cars of 1938 stock and 21 x 7-cars of Standard tube stock inclusive of spares. Because of the war, however, the actual service levels on all lines were reduced with the Winter timetables of 1939 so that the Bakerloo only had 30 trains of 1938 stock and 21 trains of Standard stock. Also, because the platform lengthening works were incomplete by the changeover date, all the trains were of 6-cars, not 7 as planned.

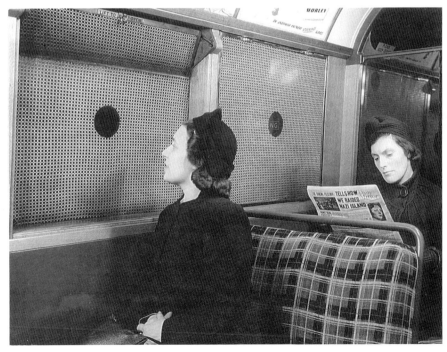

Protective netting with just a small aperture for passengers to see where they were was glued to the windows of buses and trains early in the war, as seen in this car of 1938 stock. LT Museum

Some of the Bakerloo stock transferred from the Northern already arrived as 6-car trains with NDM removed. It had actually run on the Northern in 6-car formation because of the closing of the under-river tunnels between Strand and Kennington and Moorgate and London Bridge. The closures took place during the first week of September 1939 and lasted until December 1939 in the case of the Charing Cross line and May 1940 for the City branch. Concrete plugs were inserted at the ends of the under-river sections and floodgates installed as a precaution against bomb damage.

The introduction of 6-car trains was necessary on the Strand section because the works restricted the platform length there. A number of 1938 trains had their NDMs removed and stored at Edgware and Golders Green during this period. When restoration of the normal service allowed the 7-car formations to be reinstated, some were provided by newly delivered 4-car units and the 6-car trains were transferred to the Bakerloo minus their NDMs. Records suggest that at least 10 trains went to the Bakerloo in this manner.

Some trains were reinstated at Golders Green and a complicated series of manoeuvres was carried out in an attempt to get NDMs into units which had similar mileages. Of course, all the coupling had to be done in the shops since the semi-permanent couplers could only be got at from under the car.

The Bakerloo Standard stock train formations were made up with 3 motor cars and 3 trailers in each train instead of the usual 2 motors and 4 trailers. This was largely done to overcome uncoupling problems on the Watford service but also helped to match standard stock performance with 1938 stock performance. As the war dragged on the old formation gradually returned and 1938 stock trains had their NDMs removed and replaced by trailers made spare by service reductions and the abandonment of 9-car operation on the Northern Line.

One part of the Bakerloo work which had not been completed by the changeover date was the provision of platform train describers. Only those passengers fortunate or observant enough to see the destination sign on the front of the train could be sure of whether it was destined for the Watford line or for the Stanmore line. Complaints poured in and, from December 1939, all trains for the Stanmore line had a large 'M' placed in the front cab window to help identify those trains working over the Metropolitan Line. Originally an 'S' had been proposed until it was realised that 'S' for Stanmore did not cater for trains reversing at Wembley Park. Another small problem arose when it was realised that no emergency coupling equipment had been provided for 1938 stock working on the Watford line. It had always been the practice to provide a special coupling pedestal and bar on Bakerloo stock working north of Queens Park so that a full-sized LMS train could be used to push out a defective tube train. These were eventually provided and one wonders if the corporate memory was jogged by a stalled train on the Watford line which trapped an LMS train behind it and caused a ruffling of feathers at Euston. No such incident is recorded but the first notification of the

omission was in June 1939, just after 1938 stock began working to Watford.

The Watford service had always been the odd man out as far as the London Underground was concerned. It was regarded as a joint operation between the London Underground and the main line railway, at first the LNWR and, from 1923, the LMS. The original rolling stock was jointly owned by the two companies and a 4-car or 6-car method of train operation was adopted. The basic formation was 4-cars, with two cars added at the north end to make up a 6-car train. This arrangement was changed to 3-car plus 3-car working when the original Watford Joint Stock was replaced by Standard tube stock in 1931. The overhaul and modification programmes of the New Works plans were not equipped to cope with such variations and the uncoupling of Watford trains ceased for a time during 1938 while control trailers were in works for modifications. The extra mileage generated led to the Operating Department suggesting that new stock could be used in 3+3 or 4+2 formations to allow uncoupling to recommence.

This idea was refused on the grounds that 4+2 would involve a 2-car unit with no compressor and a 3-car unit 'it is assumed . . would not be acceptable to the LMS . . .'. No record can be found as to why this latter statement was made. It is interesting to note, however, that 3-car working of 1938 stock was specifically eliminated from the Northern Line in a timetable notice of 6th February 1939. In it, the practice of using 3-car units of 1938 stock in passenger service was stopped. Hitherto, uncoupling of trains after peak hours to allow 3-car or 4-car trains to operate had been indiscriminate in both the type of stock used and which end of which type of stock was allowed to remain in service. During the off-peak periods both 3-car and 4-car sets of Standard stock were used on the Northern and the introduction of 1938 stock at first changed nothing.

There were soon found to be problems, however. Although 3-car trains of Standard stock had only one air compressor (on the motor car), 4-car trains had two. This arrangement was perfectly acceptable since the compressors were reliable and had given little trouble over many years of service. However, the 1938 stock compressors were of a new design and they did give trouble. They were specifically designed to fit under a tube car floor and were smaller than the traditional Underground type but were still expected to provide the same capacity. They weren't up to it and could not be guaranteed to maintain the necessary air pressure on the train.

To overcome the trouble a new timetable was introduced in February 1939. This eliminated the working of 3-car trains of new stock in passenger service. It was designed so that the service on the Northern was worked by 38 x 7-cars of 1938 stock, 59 x 7-cars of Standard stock and 4 x 9-cars of standard stock. New stock was only allowed to run in workings where the 3-car portion was uncoupled and stabled and the 4-car portion remained in service. Bearing in mind that this now required that all 1938 trains had to be worked with the 4-car unit at the north end and 41 trains of Standard stock having the 3-car at the north end and the remainder with the 3-car at the south end, and the constant use of a loop at Kennington, the depot foremen's jobs at Golders Green and Morden must have been close to a nightmare when it came to forming up the service each morning.

It could also be that the problems of running 3-car trains of 1938 stock were already known to the LMS and that was the reason why it was assumed that they would not want them on the Watford line. Anyway, it never came to that. The 1938 stock was not uncoupled on the Bakerloo until after World War II and Standard tube stock continued to provide short train workings when required.

Modification and Storage

In 1938, with the New Works Programme of 1935-40 then in full swing, the planned extensions progressing and much new rolling stock being built, plans for the allocation of rolling stock proposed that the flat-fronted units would be relegated to shuttle work on the Epping-Ongar service. In the event, it turned out that they were not to fulfill this particular role for another 19 years. The 18 streamlined motor cars would continue in service on the Piccadilly Line, but it was intended that each six-car train would be lengthened to seven cars by the addition of a trailer in one two-car unit of each train. Three trailers of 1938 tube stock were specially ordered for this purpose, 012412-4, and were to be delivered without compressors. With the coming of the war, these plans were not to materialise, as we shall see.

The three flat-fronted units continued in service until about September 1940, when they were put into store at Cockfosters Depot. The streamlined cars' story is a little more involved, as they received an overhaul at Acton Works. At about this time, the normal interval between overhauls was extended from every 150,000 miles to 200,000 miles, or about every four years, the (then) current paint life. The reason for the 1935 stock overhaul now seems obscure.

Five of the units did not work in service again after overhaul, eventually being stored. It is thought that those that did work in service after overhaul did so

only until about September or October 1940, although there were still four paths in the timetable for them to operate. It was apparently difficult for all but the BTH train to be kept in service. Prior to overhaul, the BTH train was split into three units to operate with the others, so that one BTH unit was thus available for three trains. With one BTH set in a train, there was a good chance that it would get home to Northfields Depot without failing in service! The technical troubles meant that it took valuable manpower to make sure that the trains were serviceable and permission was sought for all 24 cars to be stored. The official date of storing all the cars of 1935 stock is given in records as 16th May 1942, although in practice they were stored much earlier.

By early 1941, the message seems to have gone home that the train crews did not like the streamlined cab layout. A proposal was put forward to redesign two cabs of the streamlined type, so that the driver was on the conventional left hand side. Provision was also made for the driver to be able to drive the train standing up, something he could not do with the original layout but which was often necessary to ease the discomfort occasioned by being seated during long trips of up to 1½ hours. These alterations were carried out slowly during 1941-42 and the finished job, done on cars 10004 and 11004, was shown to train drivers' representatives on 21st May 1942. The only external difference was in the cab windows, which were extended up into the roof dome. The intention was that, subject to the drivers' agreement with the new design, the two modified cars would run at each end of a block train with cars 10002, 11002, 10006 and 11006. All six cars had GEC equipment, so matters must have improved with this equipment for it to be allowed to run without the protection of a PCM unit. The proposal was academic anyway, because the trainmen rejected the modifications on the grounds that the guard's position was too cramped and the side cab door let in draughts.

Meanwhile, three of the remaining cars were used as air raid protection shelters, one at Northfields and two at Cockfosters. They were sandbagged over a pit

On the left in this picture taken towards the end of the Second World War is the cab modification carried out on streamlined cars 10004 and 11004 in 1941/2. Unpopular with staff, it never worked in passenger service in this form.
John H. Meredith

road at the end where steps down were provided and used initially for sheltering until proper A.R.P. shelters could be provided. Eventually, all the cars were stored at Cockfosters Depot. By this time, it had been decided that they would not run again in their original form, and thus the proposal for them to run as seven-car trains was dropped.

Early Design Problems

It is rarely, if ever, that a new rolling stock design can enter service without teething troubles. The 1938 stock was no exception and, in fact, it was to be expected that such a radical change in existing standards would take some time to settle down. The expectations were fully justified. As we have already seen, there were some problems soon after the cars entered service and these continued for many years. During the early years of its life, the 1938 stock had over 1000 modifications. Those who might be concerned today that modifications to new trains run towards the 200 mark may take heart that the cry 'we never had this trouble with the old stock' was not necessarily true.

We have seen how there were problems with doors and bogies but there were many others. Some were relatively uninteresting to any but a specialist engineer, such as changing door valves and door interlocks and putting in a new design of retarder relay, except that the work delayed the stock's entry into service and caused much changing of unit formations. This was particularly so when the cars had to be lifted off their bogies to replace the brake cylinders or change broken motor nose suspension brackets. The brake cylinders were a big problem during the early days until a correct size could be determined. The first few trains had cylinders which were too big. They produced too large a braking force for the new type of brake block used. Later cars had smaller cylinders when delivered but even they were not right and, before half the cars were delivered, a third type was in use. Earlier cars had new cylinders fitted. There was also much changing of block types.

There was also trouble with the traction equipment. The camshaft design was such that none of the contactors were supposed to open whilst carrying current but some were found to have burnt tips. The design had to be modified to eliminate this as far as possible but it was only completely overcome by the provision of extra contactors on later PCM equipments such as those supplied for the 1949 stock and the R stock. PCM oil leaked from the cylinders and there were many cases of broken sight glasses. The gauges were all eventually replaced, after the war, by a nut carrying a glass insert.

A feature of the PCM control system was the sequence indicator. This was a light in the cab which lit when all the equipments on the train had notched up to full parallel. It went out as soon as any equipment switched off as, for example, when the train passed over a current rail gap. The constant switching of these lamps led to failures in service which were regarded by the drivers as a symptom of a defective motor car. Eventually, they became so troublesome that the majority of them were removed. The idea had

formed that perhaps it was better not to tell the drivers anything which they didn't need to know. After all, any driver worth the name would soon be able to detect by the feel of his train that all was not well. He had no need of a lamp.

Lamps in the cab became a contentious issue for the 1938 stock. As originally installed, there were three, roughly in a column on the left side of the driver's window. From the top they were for sequence, MG on and a gauge light. All were regarded as too bright and improvised steps were soon taken to reduce the brightness in the form of toffee wrappers stuck or wedged over the lamp glasses. Later, the glasses were changed to a blue tint to reduce the glare.

Originally, the stock was fitted with speedometers but they were notoriously unreliable. An instruction was issued in 1941 that they should all be covered over so that they could not be seen by the crews. The instruction was never fully carried out and in 1954 all the speedometers on the 15 trains then working on the Piccadilly were removed to provide spares for the Northern and Bakerloo. Those on the Piccadilly were deemed unnecessary since the crews were used to working without them on the Standard stock. By the early 1960s, the battle to keep them working was regarded as lost and many of them were finally blanked off. However, working examples were to be seen for many years afterwards. A trial was carried out on the Northern Line in 1958 with a new type of speedometer which was fitted to twelve cabs.

Many of the modifications necessitated uncoupling the cars. This was not the simple matter it had always been. Pre-1935 cars had Ward couplers, simple mechanical couplers which coupled on contact but which needed a man with a pole to uncouple them. He used the pole to release the clutches and then disconnected four jumpers and two hoses. To eliminate the wear and potential sources of failure of all these bits and pieces, Graff-Baker introduced the semi-permanent coupling. A steel bar, formed into a sort of elongated tray, connected the two cars and the jumpers and hoses were strapped on it. All this had to be undone to part the cars.

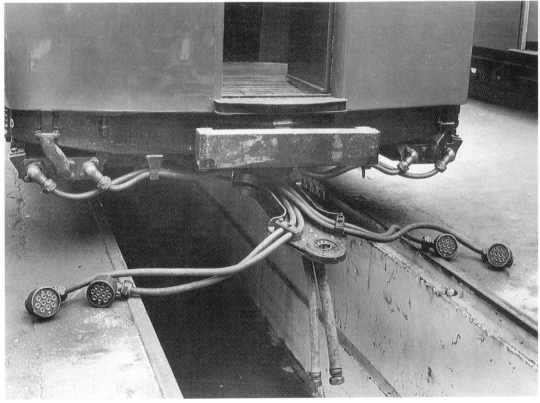

The depots did not like the idea. They had been used to quick uncoupling and easy swapping round of cars at the slightest excuse. Now it was different. They used the constant modifications to cars as an excuse to demonstrate the difficulties of uncoupling and they still swapped cars from unit to unit just as they had done before. They were, however, under strict orders to keep motor cars with corresponding numbers in the same unit, e.g. 11012 and 10012.

Those familiar with Underground train operation will know that from 1938 a system of 'unit isolation' was introduced. Any train of 1938 or later stock which develops a serious defect can be divided into two halves at the middle coupling point – pneumatically by means of air isolating cocks or electrically with a Fault Isolating Switch (F.I.S.). When isolation is completed, the good unit is used to push or pull the defective unit to the depot for repair.

On pre-1938 stocks this operation was done on a car basis. Every car had air cocks at each end for pneumatic isolation, while electrical isolation was achieved by physically removing the control jumper between the cars. The 1935 stock, although the prototype for the 1938 stock, retained the isolating cocks between cars and had a special lever at the trailing end of each car which, when operated, pulled out the jumper head from its socket far enough to break the electrical connections, but not far enough to remove the head completely.

When first delivered, the 1938 stock also had angle cocks. They were mounted on the headstock near the outside corners of the body. Unfortunately they collected water which condensed in the air piping and during cold weather it froze and split the unions. The cocks were soon removed and replaced by 'bottle traps' which collected the water and which had to be drained during maintenance examinations. They were fitted with tiny 'pet cocks' specially for this purpose.

Wartime Use

In October 1939, one month after the start of the War, new winter timetables were introduced with cuts in train services. On the Northern, 11 trains were withdrawn and on the Bakerloo, 3 trains. Delivery of the new stock continued, however, and work on overhauls was carried on at Acton. After a few months, as modification work on cars began to impinge upon the commissioning programme, cars were delivered and then stored or, in many cases, delivered, commissioned and then set aside awaiting modifications.

By the middle of 1941, when the situation had been stabilised for some time, the allocation of 1938 stock was as follows:

Line	Service	Spare Cars	Total
Northern	96 x 7	96	768
Bakerloo	27 x 6	24	186
Stored 35 TS	–	24	24
Stored 38 TS	–	198	198
Outstanding	–	27	27

The use of the term 'stored' could be taken to mean several different situations. In the case of the 1935 stock they were left, in the open, in Cockfosters Depot and remained there, unloved and, for the most part untouched, until after the war.

Of the 198 'stored' 1938 cars, 94 had not yet entered service and 104 had been commissioned and most, but by no means all, of these had run some miles in passenger service. The Northern's train services, so drastically cut in 1939, were increased by 7 trains for the Barnet extension opening in April 1940. The Bakerloo, with a planned service to Stanmore and Watford of 47 trains ran 43 or 44 until traffic built up to such a level south of Baker Street that a near full service was restored for the winter of 1941-2.

The story of the Bakerloo service during this period is interesting. It is easy to be wise after the event but there is no doubt that a serious planning error occurred during the early years of the New Works Programme. The problem of the Metropolitan's bottleneck south of Finchley Road, where four tracks became reduced to two, was intended to be solved by building two extra tracks between Finchley Road and Baker Street. The connection of these tracks to the Bakerloo and the provision of two services through to the West End and Elephant from Watford and Stanmore, instead of solving the problem, merely took the bottleneck further south. Instead of it being between Finchley Road and Baker Street, it was now between Baker Street and Elephant. This situation remained until the opening of the Jubilee Line in 1979 and the return of the Bakerloo to its original form.

From the opening to Stanmore, the increase in Bakerloo patronage continued steadily throughout the war. Although the mid-1942 service called for 27 x 6-car 1938 trains (plus 4 spare trains) and 19 x 6-car trains of Standard stock (plus 16 spare cars) there were considerable operating problems. The platform lengthening works at Elephant, difficult because of the crossover there, had not been completed and precluded the use of 7-car trains. Also the use of Standard stock, with its smaller passenger capacity and lower acceleration, led to constant disruption of the service during rush hours.

The operating department was most anxious to replace as many Standard stock trains with 1938 stock as it could. Constant pressure was applied to Acton to get more cars into passenger service but wartime conditions made this difficult. The Bakerloo could now actually muster 36½ x 6-car trains of 1938 stock but some cars were missing parts or awaiting modifications and not all could be used. To help out, a block of 5 x 6-cars was transferred from the Northern Line (together with a spare motor car) in February 1943 and all but 6 or 7 cars of the existing 'stopped' Bakerloo stock were made operational during the summer of that year.

In spite of this progress the overcrowding and delays continued. The winter of 1943 saw 41½ trains of 1938 stock available for the Bakerloo. Not all were run in service at once because some were required for normal maintenance work, but 33 or 34 could be in service at peak times and often were. It was proposed to improve on this by replacing more Standard stock cars with 1938 cars.

The first positive steps taken to use up some of the stored 1938 cars were a result of the pressure on the Bakerloo capacity south of Baker Street. Apart from 30 or so NDMs which were stored at Neasden and Stanmore awaiting the introduction of 7-car trains and a few other types in various stages of disrepair, there were no cars available for increasing capacity on the Bakerloo. However, there was a considerable number of stored or unused cars elsewhere on the system. They were listed in various depot returns as follows:

Location	Cars	Total
Golders Green	DMs	13
Golders Green	Trailers	4
Highgate	DMs	9
Edgware	DMs	20
Morden	Trailers	5
Cockfosters	Trailers	11
Acton	Trailers	2
Hammersmith	Trailers	5
Bakerloo	NDMs	30
Bakerloo	DMs	1
Bakerloo	Trailers	4
Northern	NDMs	10
Unknown	NDMs	9
Unknown	Various	12
Total		135

No more definite information on the locations or number of cars stored has come to light.

It was decided to use as many of the stored cars as possible for increasing the capacity of the Bakerloo. A total of 17 x 3-car units was therefore made up to replace an equal number of Standard stock cars. This allowed 8½ more 1938 stock trains on the Bakerloo but a considerable amount of work was necessary to achieve this.

To make up the 17 units needed, a total of 34 driving motor cars and 17 trailers was required. They were all stored, none having been commissioned because of non-delivery of traction motors, compressors and some sundry smaller items. The motor cars were sent from Golders Green (5), Highgate (9) and Edgware (20) to Acton where they were overhauled and fitted with motors removed from stored NDMs. The trailers came from Cockfosters (11), Morden (5) and Acton (1) and all but three of them were of the 092000 series purchased for use in 9-car trains. The 9-car scheme had been abandoned because of the war and the trailers stored. They were not quite the same as the 012000 series trailers and had to have some minor wiring modifications to suit their use of 6-car trains. They also went to Acton for overhaul and, when transferred to the Bakerloo, had the 'O' prefix replaced by an 'A' so that they became A92000 cars. The first of the new units entered service on 23rd February 1944 and the last on 27th July. There were now 49 x 6-car 1938 type trains available for service on the Bakerloo. Up to 42 were used in service.

By this time the end of the war was in sight. Plans were being drawn up for the future and hopes for an early peace were high. Traffic on the Underground was growing and the pressure still continued on the Bakerloo. The war did not end until May 1945 (in Europe) but, in anticipation of the event, some planning steps were taken to relieve further the pressure on the peak-hour Bakerloo service. Completion of the platform lengthening was authorised and a plan to increase all Bakerloo trains to 7-cars was drawn up.

It was proposed to increase all 49 1938 trains to 7 cars by inserting a non-driving-motor into each train. As shown in the list above, enough of them were available around the system but all were out of service and had been stored for varying periods. Most of them were without motors or compressors, having had them removed for spares or for use on the 17 units made up for the Bakerloo in 1944, and all were in need of overhaul. Of the 49 cars required, 16 had never run in service and 9 out of that 16 had never even been commissioned. The remainder had all run in service to a greater or lesser extent, some managing to run up to 50,000 miles – equivalent to a year's service.

All the cars were sent to Acton. There they were equipped with whatever equipment was missing, including motors, and were given an overhaul. In some cases the cars had been quite extensively 'robbed'. That is not to say that the missing equipment had been stolen, rather that it had been removed for use on other cars to replace defective items. The term 'robbed' was, and still is, used to denote removal of car-mounted equipment for use as spares.

When the war ended, the platform lengthening and car overhaul work began. By the winter timetable of 1945, twenty-five trains had been lengthened and work continued all through the next year. Progress was delayed by post-war shortages and by some confusion during the early days over which way the trains should be formed.

It had always been the custom on the Bakerloo to detach the north end of the train for uncoupling purposes. This went back to pre-1930 days when the 2-car north end unit was uncoupled from a 6-car Watford train to leave a 4-car train working the off-peak service. However, when the 7-car formation was introduced on the Bakerloo, the first few trains were made up with the 4-car unit (containing the NDM) at the north end and the 3-car unit at the south end.

At that time there was no uncoupling on the tube lines. It had been suspended during the war and was not yet reinstated. Seeing that the New Works Programme had not been completed and was already in complete disarray as regards rolling stock allocation, including the extra 1938 stock on the Bakerloo, it was to be some time before it was reintroduced. However, the thinking at the time was that it would soon restart. People were anxious to return to pre-war conditions. Some fears were expressed then, when it was discovered that the 4-car units were being run at the north end of trains. After the operating department had suggested a mixture of both 4 + 3 and 3 + 4 formations and had been overruled by the CME, it was decided to run the trains with the 3-car unit at the north end. They therefore became: North, DM – T – DM + DM – T – NDM – DM, South.

Chapter 4
Post-War Plans

Even though the Bakerloo had already had three successive injections of new rolling stock it had long been the operating department's intention to eliminate Standard stock from the line completely. It had been and still was, proving difficult to run a small number of slower, older and effectively smaller trains between faster trains of 1938 stock. Between three and five trains of Standard stock were running each day during peak periods and occasionally 6-car trains of 1938 stock were run in place of 7-car trains. Three more units of 1938 stock were made up using some stored cars and two trailers of the 27 outstanding cars which were delivered in 1946. These units entered service in July 1947. They were done to allow the release of some more Standard stock cars for use on the Central Line. The extensions to Woodford and Newbury Park were opened in December 1947 and the Standard cars released were needed for the new services.

Although it was hoped to continue preparing stored and newly delivered 1938 stock (the 27 outstanding cars were all delivered between June 1946 and July 1947) the Central Line extensions took precedence and, from October 1947, all work on 1938 stock stopped apart form normal overhauls. A lot of work was concentrated on rehabilitation of stored Standard stock to try and get it into working order for use on the Central Line. Meanwhile, there was a hiatus for the 1938 stock which remained virtually unchanged for almost two years. The remaining newly delivered 1938 cars were stored, mostly at Hammersmith depot, awaiting a final decision as to their use. In the meantime various schemes for the future allocation of rolling stock were being drawn up.

Post-war plans for the 1938 stock were based on the current fleet totals of:

24	1935 experimental DMs
644	1938 DMs
206	1938 NDMs
58	58 Trailers
271	1938 Trailers
1203	Total

Some 27 cars of 1938 stock were not delivered until after the Second World War. Here a set of four trailers are seen about to leave Birmingham for London in August 1946. HRMS Collection

1938 tube stock approaches Hendon on a southbound Kennington train in the late 1940s. LT Museum

An initial look at what was required compared with what was available revealed some interesting ideas. To begin with, the New Works Programme was still regarded as viable but with modifications to fit the changed circumstances. The Central Line extensions were going ahead, minus the West Ruislip to Denham section which had already become a casualty before the war in a cost-cutting exercise. The Northern Line extensions were partly finished and were held in abeyance pending a go-ahead from the government. The real problem (as far as following stock allocation was concerned) was the Bakerloo. Instead of having 34 trains of 1938 stock and 20 trains of Standard stock, as originally planned, all 54 trains were to be of 1938 stock.

A note of caution to the reader here. It is nowadays customary to allot trains to each line on the basis of a number required for service plus spare *units* required for maintenance. Although trains of 1938 stock were formed into 3-car and 4-car units and exact 7-car trains were purchased for spares, it was still the practice in the immediate post-war years to calculate the spares on a *car* basis, even though this gave rise to odd cars being available in the depot. It was this which allowed odd spares to show in the Bakerloo figures mentioned earlier in this story and which also appear in the rolling stock allocations required in 1947:

Northern service: 100 x 7 cars + 100 spares = 800 cars
Bakerloo service: 47 x 7 cars + 47 spares = 376 cars

Neither the spares allocation on the Northern, nor that on the Bakerloo allowed the formation of a batch of standard units. Neither could the full requirements for this allocation of cars be met from the existing stock. Although there were 1179 cars available (the 1935 stock is excluded) and only 1176 were required in the above table, the split of car types was wrong. This arose because of the original plan to run 9 and 6-car trains of the stock as well as 7-car trains. The final figures showed that there were 10 DM cars short of requirements. Only 644 were available and 654 were required. Various schemes were therefore proposed for the redeployment of the stock.

It was assumed that there would not be a return to 9-car train operation. It was a scheme which 'seemed like a good idea at the time' but the post-war conditions did not really lend themselves to a resumption. It was basically too expensive to run, too difficult to operate and too much work was involved in getting it going again. This threw up a batch of non-standard cars which would need special consideration in any new programme. The 24 cars of 1935 Stock also needed consideration. They made up 4 x 6-car trains, one of which was originally planned to be used on the Central Line to provide shuttle services at the eastern end while the other three were to go to the Piccadilly, increased to 7-car trains by the addition of a 1938 trailer. Three trailers were specially ordered for this purpose. As already noted, they differed from other 1938 trailers in not having a compressor because it was already provided on the 11000 series motor cars of 1935 stock.

First proposals suggested the conversion of the 18 streamlined 1938 stock cars to trailers for use with Standard stock trains on the Piccadilly while retaining the 6 flat-ended cars for the Central Line shuttle. It was proposed to scrap all but the BTH traction equipment on these cars and put it on the flat-ended cars in place of their MV equipment. Then a further scheme proposed the transfer of the three streamlined trains, with their 1938 trailers, to the Bakerloo to go towards eliminating Standard stock from there. Although no mention was made of it at the time, they would presumably have been re-equipped with BTH traction control purchased specially for the purpose. Neither of these schemes took account of the 1938 stock position nor of what was to be done about the erstwhile 9-car trains.

Block Trains

The reader will recall that 10 x 9-car trains were ordered as part of the 1938 stock fleet. Late in 1938, the LPTB was so anxious to get these trains into service that they asked the car builders to concentrate on them in preference to the Standard vehicles. Consequently, the first cars of this special batch were delivered in February 1939 and the last in May. Unfortunately, the pressure of the New Works train overhaul programme and the special design requirements of some of the cars in the block trains caused a crisis.

The need for Standard stock cars to be overhauled for the Central Line could only be fulfilled by transferring cars away from the Northern Line to Acton Works. They had to be replaced by 1938 stock going into service. The introduction of 9-car trains was therefore essential to keep up the flow of cars to Acton for overhaul, and there was a delay in the delivery of some of these new cars which caused a crisis. The cars in question were the Special NDMs for the 9-car trains, which had the guard's door control panels. To overcome the problem on a short-term basis some 7-car 'block' trains were put into service. These were standard 1938 stock trains but they used middle DM cars whose guard's door controls had not yet been fitted. Although they were fitted later, for the time being these cars could not be used on trains required to uncouple. They were returned to standard after June 1939 when the first of the 9-car trains appeared.

The idea of 'block' trains was not new to the 1938 stock. It arose as a result of the practice of uncoupling. The use of long trains during peak hours and short trains during off-peak hours was as old as the Underground itself. All the original trains were made to be split into smaller portions with a cab at each end for use as short trains. Coupling and uncoupling in service was a standard feature of Underground timetables and it was planned that the 1938 stock would also uncouple on a regular basis.

A result of uncoupling was the development of the block train. Trains to be uncoupled had to be made up of the right number and type of cars all in the right position in each train. The location of cars with cabs was particularly important. However, if a train was not to be uncoupled, i.e. it was only required to run during the peaks, a degree of flexibility could be allowed in its formation as long as it met the performance requirements. In the classic Standard stock example, trailers were used in place of control trailers and vice versa. Such trains were known as block trains. For the 1938 stock, the 7-car trains which ran temporarily without door controls fitted to the middle DM cars were the first example of the 1938 stock 'block' train, i.e. one which could not be uncoupled to form two short trains. They were certainly not to be the last. The 9-car trains were also a block formation.

Enough cars of the type needed for the 9-car formation had been commissioned by the first week of May 1939 to allow a test run. On the 8th, a night-time run from Golders Green to Kennington revealed that some signals at Leicester Square and Charing Cross needed to be repositioned. Much work had already been done on signalling in 1937 when the original 9-car trains began running but these were, of course, formed of Standard stock and it was found that 1938 stock was slightly longer than Standard stock. While the signalling alteration work was being arranged, the critical stock position led to the introduction of another of what was to become a series of block train formations of 1938 stock.

This block train formation was made up by removing the trailers from a 9-car train. As this left 7 cars which were all motor cars, the traction equipment was isolated, the motor brushes were removed and covers were fitted to the traction motor vents on two of the NDM cars. Whilst it may, at first glance, seem strange

A Watford train enters Willesden Junction station on 4th July 1953. Services to Watford were reduced to peak hours only in 1966 and were withdrawn completely in 1982. Alan A. Jackson

to remove the trailers and then effectively convert two NDMs to trailers (even though they still had all their redundant traction equipment to drag around) it was the only sensible solution. The original 9-car formation was:

$$1 \quad 2 \quad 3 \quad 4 \quad 5 \quad 6 \quad 7 \quad 8 \quad 9$$
$$DM-NDM\times SNDM-T-NDM-T-SNDM+NDM-DM$$

(SNDM = Special NDM with guard's position;
x = Ward coupler)

A look at this formation quickly demonstrates the situation. The question to be answered is which cars should be removed to give a 7-car train with the same performance as a proper 7-car train. The DMs must be kept for the driver's cabs and the SNDMs for the guard's controls. The end NDMs in positions 2 and 8 could go but they had Ward couplers at one end which would leave the SNDM to couple with the DM. The coupler incompatibility was not worth correcting for what was intended only to be a temporary arrangement. This left the middle NDM or the trailers. Taking out the middle NDM and one other car left an asym-

metrical formation which left the guard's position in the wrong place. It therefore had to be the trailers.

The trains therefore were formed in this manner:

$$1 \quad 2 \quad 3 \quad (5) \quad 7 \quad (8) \quad 9$$
$$DM-NDM \times SNDM - NDM - SNDM \times NDM - DM$$

(The cars with position numbers in brackets had their traction equipment isolated.)

Three of them entered service on the Northern Line on 15th May 1939 and covered the workings of three 9-car trains. With continued pressure on the operating department to accept more of these trains and even to put 9-car trains into service before the signalling work was done, an agreement was reached in June 1939 to run a total of 8 x 7-car block trains and 2 x 9-car trains. The 9-car trains were to have the end doors sealed closed until the signalling alterations were completed. They entered service on 19th June 1939 and the remaining 5 x 7-car block trains were added to the three already in service by 26th June.

Although mention was made earlier of some of the features of the 9-car trains which differed from conventional 1938 stock trains, it is worthwhile recording some of the peculiarities of these trains, particularly as they also affected the 7-car block trains derived from them.

To begin with, the cars were specially numbered on the solebars from 1 to 9 consecutively starting at the 'A' end of the train. These numbers survived on the 7-car block trains as well. The emergency coupling points between cars 2 & 3 and 7 & 8 had the Ward couplers fitted wrong way up with the release lever underneath instead of on top. The jumpers and hoses were arranged for withdrawal from under the train. The arrangement caused a lot of trouble – imagined if not real – when it was suggested in 1945 that the hoses should be moved up to waist level to make emergency uncoupling easier. This was done and many of the altered cars retained the mounting plates at waist level even after conversion to standard cars in the early 1950s.

There were only two drivers' and two guards' positions on the whole 9-car train, compared to four on the conventional 7-car train. The drivers' cabs were, not unnaturally, on cars 1 and 9 while the guards' positions were at the outer ends of cars 3 and 7, the Special NDMs (SNDM). Handbrakes were provided at each of these positions, the driver's being the lever type introduced for the 1938 stock; the guard's being a lockable rotary device, the locking facility being considered necessary as it was in the passenger saloon.

The door controls were interesting. A special box was provided on the roof at the guard's position. This contained push buttons and indicator lights to give 'front cars cut in' or 'rear cars cut in' as required. At a platform which could accommodate a whole 9-car train (only those north of Hampstead), both buttons were operated and all doors opened. At 7-car platforms the guard operated whichever button was necessary to get the correct doors to open. On occasions when the rear cars were stopped within the platform at tunnel stations the leading door of car 3 was in the tunnel as well as the two front cars. This door remained closed when other doors on the car opened.

The door control system was quite complex and it relied on the guard to get things right to avoid doors being opened on cars in the tunnel. The Ministry of Transport was a little nervous of the scheme in its early days when Standard stock was used and they asked if a 'photo-eye' could be used to detect the train's location and prevent the wrong door opening. This was regarded as too complex (rightly so) and the LPTB offered to put a barrier rail along tunnel walls near platforms to prevent a passenger falling out and under the train if the doors were opened in error. This was accepted.

Naturally, when 7-car block trains were formed, all these special features remained even though all cars were always within the platforms. They were regarded as a nuisance by the guards, particularly as they were used to working on normal trains and only rarely worked block trains. In later years, as we shall see, there were many modifications which attempted to overcome some of the objections but which actually caused more problems.

Although they were only in service for a couple of months, a problem quickly developed with the 9-car trains. Their current consumption was very high, some 4500 amps during acceleration. It was therefore arranged to run them in 'Forward 1', the lower rate of acceleration. This reduced the current to 3680 amps and thus solved the problem. Quite what would happen when all the planned 9-car trains were in service was not considered and, as it turned out, was never found out. They ceased running in September 1939, withdrawn because of the difficulties of running them in the blackout, and were never run in that formation again. The two trains concerned had their trailers removed and were run as block trains like the eight already formed.

The block trains ran throughout the year. When victory for the Allies seemed only a matter of time, thoughts towards renewing pre-war plans began to take shape. In November 1944, Graff-Baker calculated that with 14 more DMs, 14 more trailers and an additional NDM he could make the former 10 x 9-car trains into 17 x 7-car trains if the LPTB did not want to resume 9-car train operations. They did not. This was finally decided early in 1946 but it was clear from a report written in June 1939 that 9-car operation had a limited usefulness:

'An investigation of loadings shows that on only four of the sixteen trips does the number of passengers exceed that which might comfortably be accommodated in a standard 7-car train.

'Special observations showed that 9-car trains do not at present affect the running to an undue extent. It was, however, noticeable that following trains were slightly checked on many occasions, which should serve as a warning that a great increase in the number of 9-car trains in service might have unfortunate repercussions on running generally.

'Special features of 9-car operation include shunting movements at Golders Green on the southbound road, as the trains are too long to be accommodated in the shunting neck, complication in platform work at Edgware, as only No. 1 platform can hold them, and erection of special moveable signs on platforms, as the extra cars cannot be permanently labelled under present conditions. Moreover, these trains cannot be diverted to other sections of the line in case of emergency.

'There seems to be a general impression that, although the practicability of 9-car trains has been proved, an extension of the principle to make these trains the standard peak hour stock would not be desirable. Such extension would involve very heavy capital expenditure, a strengthening of power supply, and, probably, many or all of the central area platforms would require lengthening. Moreover, Camden Junction might need reconstruction at very great expense. It seems preferable therefore to concentrate on the extension and simplification of the running of a limited number of these trains on carefully selected paths during peak hours.'

Post-war industrial and financial restrictions plus the uncertainty over whether the New Works Programme could continue as planned, sealed the fate of 9-car trains. The original scheme was for 4 trains on the Edgware Branch and 4 on the Barnet branch with 2 spare trains. Only 2 of the 1938 stock trains ever ran as 9-car sets and the Barnet line never saw them. A scheme to run them through to Morden never came to fruition either. They never ran south of Kennington.

As the 9-car train concept had been officially abandoned, any programme for new cars had to take into account the mis-match of cars which resulted. The scheme to reform the 9-car stock assumed that block trains were to continue. If they were, they would not be capable of being uncoupled. If uncoupling was resumed, were some block trains still suitable – confined to rush hours only – and how many could there be? The question of uncoupling was now reviewed.

Post-War Block Trains

The Underground's long standing practice of uncoupling to provide shorter trains during off-peak hours was abandoned at the outbreak of the war principally because of the physical difficulties of coupling and uncoupling during the blackout. It was also considered desirable to have full-length trains available 'in case of emergency'. Eventually too, the shortage of staff would have led to the cancellation of uncoupling.

As soon as the war ended, an investigation into the benefits or otherwise of uncoupling was carried out. The results formed a report which is interesting in that it found that the financial benefits of uncoupling and running a given frequency of off-peak service were negated if full length trains were run all day and service intervals widened slightly because of the extra capacity available on each train. It went on to recommend that consideration be given to designing new trains without providing for uncoupling:

'From the Operating point of view, it is possible – without uncoupling – to provide trains having more doorway space for use particularly in the rush hours, as it is not necessary to sterilise parts of the train for intermediate motor cabs. Some increases in passenger carrying capacity, both seats and standing, would result from this.

'From the Engineering point of view, the absence of coupling points would (a) reduce the amount of equipment to be provided, (b) simplify it, since only such coupling devices would be fitted as would be required to couple two trains together in an emergency, and (c) the reliability of the service in operation would be increased, since circuits along the train can be made more securely by avoiding an uncoupling point and, having been made, remain more secure owing to being undisturbed.

'It is, therefore, RECOMMENDED that consideration be given to the construction of future trains in a manner not providing for uncoupling, as well as the modification – as opportunity offers – of the existing trains to the same condition.'

The recommendation was not accepted, for the time being at least. Apart from the work done to increase

the Bakerloo capacity, little else was done to 1938 stock over the next two years. Post-war material shortages and coal consumption restrictions by the government meant little was possible in the way of new stock procurement. Some preparatory research work was done however and, in February 1948, a new scheme for reorganisation of the 1938 stock and the purchase of new cars was approved.

The new programme was based on several new ideas. First, as we have seen, the Bakerloo service was to be operated entirely by 1938 stock. It was presently four trains short of this target but, by ordering the right types of cars, this could be overcome by 18 additional cars. Next, it was proposed to increase the Northern Line service to its pre-war capacity. With the Barnet line opened in the meantime, this required another 6 x 7-cars plus 7 spare cars. Finally, it was planned to increase the Piccadilly Line service following the building of a flyover at Rayners Lane and 4-tracking the line between Acton Town and Hanger Lane Junction.

This is the point at which the Northern City Line began to appear in new plans. In the New Works Programme it had been planned to use 16 cars of 1920 built Cammell-Laird stock, in trains powered by Standard stock motor cars, on the Northern City Line shuttle service between Moorgate and Finsbury Park. It was quickly discovered though, that the cars were not suitable for the platforms and these needed to be altered. Even though work was done to allow Standard tube stock to work over the line in place of the old full-size GN&C cars, the Cammell-Laird cars were still outside the normal gauge envelope.

By the end of the war, these cars were 25 years old and had been stored in the open at Cockfosters since their removal from service on the Bakerloo in 1939. They were in poor condition and were not considered worth the expense of repairing. Eventually, five of them were equipped as an instruction train for the rolling stock maintenance department and the remainder were scrapped.

The Northern City had been worked with Standard stock all through the war. As the Piccadilly Line was also worked entirely by Standard stock, it was proposed under this new programme to implement the increase in the Piccadilly service by using the Northern City Standard stock and replacing it with the 1938 stock. This would require a further 8 x 6-car trains and 12 spare cars.

The whole programme required 127 additional cars. These were to be obtained by:

Conversion of 18 streamlined 1935 cars
Absorption of 20 cars ex 9-car stock
Purchase of 89 new cars.

All the new cars were to be driving motors. It was obviously envisaged at this time that uncoupling would be re-introduced at some time quite soon, perhaps forced by the government in attempts to reduce energy consumption. With 89 new DMs combined with existing stock, all but four trains of the 1938 stock would be divisible into 3-car and 4-car units. The odd

A 4-car train of 1938 stock at Kilburn in 1950. Note the 3rd car is a '58 trailer' built in 1927. LT Museum

four trains would be of the block type; all that remained of the 10 which had run throughout the war. There would be an excess of NDMs resulting from the plan but it was to be overcome by converting 22 of them to trailers. The traction equipment removed from them was to be used on 22 of the new cars.

It was envisaged that the 4 x 7-car block trains would use the cars in four existing block trains but with 2 NDMs in each train converted to trailers and the Special NDMs moved to allow the emergency coupling points to be reduced from two to one. They were to be formed as follows:

DM – T – NDM – SNDM x SNDM – T – DM
(Ward coupler at x)

The guard's door control equipment was to be standardised and removed from the SNDMs to the usual position on the trailing ends of the driving cars. These trains were to stay on the Northern Line.

Block Trains on the Bakerloo

The new tube stock programme was agreed in the spring of 1948 and formally approved in August 1948 by the London Transport Executive, as the LPTB had become since nationalisation of the railways at the beginning of the year. Even before this approval, however, the Operating Department realised that it could get some extra trains into service before the new cars were delivered. All the 27 cars outstanding delivery since 1941 had arrived and many of them were stored at Hammersmith. By starting work at once, some extra trains, it was argued, could be formed for helping out the beleaguered Bakerloo.

By June 1948, a scheme had been drawn up. There were a number of spare DM cars available on the Bakerloo, including one which had not yet been commissioned. Trailers for them were stored at Hammersmith and there was a pair of NDMs spare as well. It

was calculated that by replacing the NDMs running as trailers in the 10 Northern Line block trains with stored trailers and forming them up with the spare DMs and more stored cars, another four block trains could be made up. Detailed plans were drawn up and extra cars were to be obtained as follows:

1 Stored DM at Neasden
7 Spare DMs at Neasden
2 Stored NDMs (1 Neasden, 1 Hammersmith)
5 Stored (9-car) trailers at Hammersmith
9 Stored trailers (delivered post war) at Hammersmith
4 Spare trailers at Golders Green

In the end, the actual cars used to form the extra trains were not all from this list. For convenience, there were some transfers of cars between the Northern and Bakerloo so that, for example, two A92XXX cars from the Bakerloo finished up in 7-car block trains on the Northern.

The original 7-car block formation on the Northern was as follows:

```
1     2      3     (5)    7    (8)    9
DM − NDM × SNDM − NDM − SNDM × NDM − DM
```

Of the 10 trains of this type, 6 remained the same except that they had a new trailer inserted in place of the middle (5) NDM thus:

```
1     2      3      7    (8)    9
DM − NDM × SNDM − T − SNDM × NDM − DM
```

The position numbers shown refer to the originally intended locations for the 9-car trains. The brackets denote NDMs running as trailers. This formation was now called 'Block Train Type I'.

The remaining four trains were split up, the additional cars were inserted and two batches of 4 x 7-car block trains were formed with one batch as below:

```
1     2      3      5      9
DM − NDM × SNDM − T − NDM − T − DM
```

This was known as Type II and used trailers which had been originally intended for use in 9-car trains. The NDMs in position 5 had their motors restored and now ran as proper NDMs. These trains were peculiar in having the guard's positions asymmetrical. The SNDM in position 3 still had a guard's position but the absence of the SNDM in position 7 meant that guard's controls had to be installed on the DMs in position 9. This was a time-consuming job and delayed the introduction of this formation until April 1949.

The final batch of 4 trains (Type III) went into service on the Bakerloo between March and June 1949 and was formed as follows:

$$5 \quad 5 \quad 7 \quad (8)$$
$$DM-T-NDM-NDM-SNDM\times NDM-DM$$

The former position 5 NDMs all had their motors restored except for two standard NDMs which came from store. The DMs were also standard but had to have wiring alterations to allow them to run in these trains.

By the early summer of 1949, the last Standard stock train was withdrawn from the Bakerloo. The ultimate had been achieved after 5 years of trying. It was not, however, to solve the problem of overcrowding on the line and it was to remain a thorn in the side of the operating department for many years to come.

Permanent Block Trains

A natural consequence of the work on increasing the 10 block trains to 14, was to ask whether the new tube stock programme could be altered to take advantage of the scheme. Apparently, it could. The original programme approved in August 1948 envisaged the purchase of 89 DMs, the conversion of the 18 streamlined cars to trailers and the conversion of 22 NDMs to trailers. With block train formations permanently in use however, the number of DM cars could be reduced, and the NDMs retained. The balance of cars was in trailers. The order therefore changed to 67 DMs and 22 Trailers.

The 1948 allocation plan for rolling stock did not change as a result of the revised order:

Northern:	106 x 7 cars + 106 spares =	848 cars
Bakerloo:	47 x 7 cars + 49 spares =	378 cars
Northern City:	8 x 6 cars + 12 spares =	60 cars
		1286 cars

It is not possible to equate these totals to train formations because it was still the practice to classify spares in cars rather than in units or trains. It was, however, stated that there would be only 13 x 7-cars of block trains and that the total number of NDMs with Ward couplers for emergency uncoupling would be 26. Ten of the trains would go on the Northern and three on the Bakerloo. All the other cars formerly in 9-car or block trains would be converted to Standard.

This plan was accepted in January 1949 and the order for the new cars, which had already been placed with Birmingham in October 1948, was amended to suit. This amendment was not to last long as there was a further reappraisal soon afterwards.

This reappraisal was really only a continuation of the ideas which had gone before. Ever since the realisation in 1945 that there was little to choose between uncoupling for off-peak periods and running full-length trains all day, Graff-Baker had had the idea that driver's cabs in the middle of trains could be dispensed with. Block trains could become universal. He now moved a step closer to this by suggesting that the 67 DM cars on order should be NDMs. They were cheaper to build than cars with cabs and the order as a whole would be less expensive because it would only require one type of car body because for the NDM and the trailer it was the same.

So, yet another rolling stock allocation programme was drawn up. This time it envisaged the provision of 47 x 7-car block trains. This figure as derived by taking the existing block trains (14) and seeing how many more could be made up with a pair of NDMs in place of the two middle DMs. The answer was 33, which gave 66 NDMs required plus a spare new one which was to be integrated into an existing block train.

Authorisation for this change, which was granted in May 1949, did not actually approve the abandonment of uncoupling. The LTE hedged its bets by noting that cars being purchased for the Camberwell extension would all have to be driving motor cars if uncoupling was to be reinstated. No one had actually said uncoupling was officially abandoned and no one had seriously asked for its resumption. In the meantime, Camberwell loomed large.

Camberwell

There had been a long cherished hope that, one day, the Bakerloo Line would be extended south from Elephant & Castle to Camberwell Green. Powers for such an extension were granted by an Act of Parliament in 1931. For one reason or another, little more was done towards actually building it, aside from some preliminary estimates of what was required in the way of rolling stock, which was calculated (in 1934) as being 55 cars of Standard stock. It was not included as part of the New Works Programme but, in 1936, it was proposed as part of a scheme for relief of the Southern Railway lines to Charing Cross and Cannon Street.

The scheme envisaged the Bakerloo being extended south to Camberwell and then east to Peckham Rye where it would rise to the surface and connect with the Southern Railway Line to Nunhead and Lewisham. It would then take over the Southern's line to Dartford via Bexleyheath. Under this plan, Bakerloo trains would have run from Watford to Dartford! It was not to be. In the hierarchy of choices for new routes being considered under the New Works Programme, it ran a poor fifth behind the four schemes adopted for North London.

By the end of the war, however, things had changed. The in-town section of the Bakerloo was under severe pressure because of the increased traffic from the Metropolitan Line and the only way the service would be increased was thought to be by an improvement in the terminal facilities at the southern end. Either Elephant had to be enlarged or a new terminus built further south, at Camberwell, for example.

In 1947 the original scheme was dusted off and re-assessed. It was proposed to build a 4-track terminus at Camberwell with twin sidings and two running tunnels beyond the station like Liverpool Street (Central Line), with a view to extending east in the future. It was assumed that the rolling stock for the Camberwell extension would be ordered separately from anything else being purchased although it would, of course, be entirely compatible with 1938 stock. An extra 98 (14 x 7) cars were estimated to be necessary for the extension service which was to include increasing the Bakerloo service from 32 to 40 trains per hour. A new depot was to be built on the site of the stabling sidings at Stanmore and the line resignalled with speed control signalling.

From 1947 to mid-1949, the planning for the Camberwell extension had been slowly progressing, in parallel with the Piccadilly improvements such as the Rayners Lane flyover, four-tracking Acton Town to Hanger Lane Junction and Ickenham Depot, which were to enable the service improvements proposed in the 1948 plan. When the national economic situation began to take a turn for the worse in the autumn of 1949, the various capital investment schemes for the Underground came under close scrutiny. As a result, the Piccadilly Line schemes were shelved and the Northern Line extension to Bushey Heath was buried forever. Only Camberwell survived – for a time at least.

The loss of the Piccadilly Line improvement schemes rebounded on the 1938 stock programme. The original intention to supply 10 x 6 car trains of 1938 stock to the Northern City Line and then transfer the displaced Standard stock to the Piccadilly to increase the service was no longer viable. There were now 60 cars, already ordered, and nowhere to put them. There was a long hard look at the 1938 stock situation.

A number of factors were taken into consideration. There was the Camberwell extension, the loss of the Piccadilly improvements, an economic crisis in the country and, most recent of all, a plan to replace all the Standard stock on the Piccadilly Line with new stock which was to be known a the 1952 tube stock. The combination of all these gave the impetus for a new plan. It was now decided that:

– the 89 new cars on order would ultimately go for the Camberwell extension
– the Northern would not get any increase in stock because the proposal to increase services to the pre-war level was abandoned.
– the Piccadilly overcrowding would be relieved by the temporary use of the 89 new cars until the arrival of the 1952 stock
– the Piccadilly Line's 89 new cars would allow some Standard stock to be transferred to the Central to lengthen some more trains there from 7-cars to 8-cars.

It was intended that the 89 cars, by now known as the 1949 tube stock, would be sufficient both for the Camberwell extension and the proposal to increase the Bakerloo service to 40 trains per hour, but only was because it was now planned to cut back the Watford service to Harrow and Wealdstone, thus releasing some stock. This allowed the new stock requirements to be reduced to 89 cars instead of the 98 originally planned for Camberwell.

As can be seen from the revised plan, the proposal to increase Northern Line services to their pre-war level had gone by the board. The government was trying to restrict coal consumption and keeping train mileage down was one way this could be done. The Northern Line never got its pre-war service back. The cancellation of this scheme and that to put 1938 stock on the Northern City, set free the 89 new cars for the new programme.

There was one problem which had to be addressed: the running on the Piccadilly Line, even as a temporary measure, of a batch of new trains amongst older stock. If the 89 new cars were to be run with Standard tube stock, a repetition of the problems previously experienced by the Bakerloo under similar, if not identical circumstances, had to be avoided. It was therefore decided to reduce the performance of the 1938 stock trains by cutting out the equipment on the NDM car. It was also proposed that the trains would be 'fleeted', i.e. they would all run together during the height of the peak period so that their greater capacity would be used to maximum effect. When the trains actually entered service on the Piccadilly however, the fleeting was rarely achieved in practice. Also, the NDMs were used with their motors working but they and the new "UNDMs" cars introduced at that time were restricted to series operation only. From August 1953, the UNDMs were restored to normal and the 'A' motor cars of 3-car units were restricted to series only.

The 1949 Tube Stock Programme

A new plan for the distribution of 1938 stock was drawn up as follows:

Northern: 100 x 7-cars + 103 spare cars = 803 cars
Bakerloo: 47 x 7-cars + 49 spare cars = 378 cars
Piccadilly: 13 x 7-cars + 14 spare cars = 105 cars

Total = 1286 cars

The Piccadilly actually got more new cars than the 89 on order because there were enough cars left over to make up 13 x 7- car trains and spares, following the cancellation of the Northern Line service improvements. Spares were still unrelated to train formations, being calculated on a car basis.

There had, until this time, been little talk of a resumption of uncoupling. The block train concept had accepted the need for emergency uncoupling by providing the easily released Ward coupler, with hoses and jumpers, at a point in the middle of the train. The uncoupling had to be done from underneath and was intended, initially, to assist in dealing with persons trapped under trains. It soon developed, with the increase in block trains, towards assisting with train repairs. It was convenient to deal with half a train which was defective rather than immobilise a whole train. The quick uncoupling allowed the easier swapping of halves of block trains.

A logical extension of the emergency coupler idea was to replace it with a fully automatic coupler. All it needed was a switch to operate it. The driving ends of the 1938 stock trains had it, so why not the non-driving ends? The idea had been applied to the District Line's R Stock, then being delivered, so it seemed sensible to apply it to tube trains.

Of course, it was an expensive item. It would increase the cost of the cars and it would increase maintenance. It might however prove to be a time saver in allowing shunting movements in depots to be completed more quickly. It would also save on staff. Uncoupling could be done by one man instead of two. The 'pole man' who had to unlatch the Ward coupler and undo the jumpers and hoses could be dispensed with. One man could operate the uncoupler switch and the units would push apart. Once this was realised, the idea quickly took hold. Work began on designing the alterations necessary to provide the couplers – the Wedglock type – for what were now being called the 'Uncoupling' non-driving motors. They were given the initials UNDM and were soon being referred to by everyone as 'Undums'.

There was a new problem associated with this scheme. If interchangeability was the goal, it could not be achieved with the present programme. If Wedglock couplers were provided on the 67 new UNDMs they would not then be compatible with the uncoupling arrangements on the existing 14 block trains. To convert all the existing block trains would have involved providing 28 more UNDMs, two for each train. One would come from the 67 on order, the other 27 converted from existing NDMs. The total number of block trains would therefore become 47, as noted earlier. There were still uneven numbers of cars left for spares, including 4 odd motor cars. Eventually, it was decided to tidy things up. By reducing the block trains

to 46 and ordering 2 more new cars to give 91 in all, an even balance of cars could be obtained giving a total of 1288 cars formed into 184 x 7-car trains. It was done as follows:

– New UNDMs ordered = 70 (three more than the 67 NDMs ordered before)
– New trailers ordered = 21 (one less than before)
– SNDMs converted to UNDMs = 20
– Ordinary NDMs converted to UNDMs = 2
– 1935 motors converted to trailers = 18

The UNDMs were to have automatic couplers and were to be fitted with motor-generators. They were now envisaged as replacements for driving motor cars. Because they had automatic couplers they became 'handed' and therefore became 'A' UNDMs or 'D' UNDMs to denote which way they faced. Block trains were to be formed as follows:

'A' DM–T–NDM–'D' UNDM+'A' UNDM–T–'D' DM

Most of these ideas concerning UNDMs were firmed up during the spring of 1950, but by the July it had finally been decided to go ahead with uncoupling on the tube lines. A new, more detailed programme was set up for the 1938 stock:

Piccadilly:	Block trains:	15 x 7-cars
Bakerloo:	Block trains:	4 x 7-cars
	3 + 4 trains:	50 x 7-cars
Northern:	Block trains:	27 x 7-cars
	3 + 4 trains:	32 x 7-cars
	4 + 3 trains:	56 x 7-cars

The block trains would all have two UNDMs in the middle. The 3 + 4 car trains had the 4-car unit at the

Newly-delivered trailer 30044 of 1949 stock. H. Luff

south end and 4 + 3 car trains had the 4-car unit at the north end. It was planned to have trains uncouple on the Northern Line so that a 7-car train would split into a 3-car train and a 4-car train. The 3-car would work via Bank, the 4-car via Charing Cross. On the Bakerloo, only 4-car units were to be used for off-peak services. All uncoupled 3-car units on that line would stable.

On the Piccadilly Line it was originally intended that the block trains would never uncouple. They were to run during peak periods only, being 'fleeted' as described earlier. However, Graff-Baker did not see the point of this and eventually persuaded everyone that it was a waste of money to have new cars sitting around doing nothing most of the day while older cars of Standard stock clocked up thousands more miles each month. It was therefore decided to allow 1938 stock trains to uncouple on the Piccadilly Line.

While this new idea completely threw out the carefully planned stock allocation programme it did, in a roundabout way, allow some money to be saved on the purchase of new equipment. The use of 3-car units as off-peak trains on the Northern Line had resurrected an old problem: They had only one air compressor. The reader will recall the pre-war problem with this which resulted in an elaborate new uncoupling schedule being introduced in February 1939 to obviate the use of 1938 stock 3-car units as service trains. To overcome the problem in the post war scheme it was decided to fit all the 'non UNDM' 3-car units on the Northern with an extra compressor. The 88 x 3-car units involved were to have 2 KLL4 compressors fitted on the trailer car. The car numbers of the trailers were to be altered so that the 'O' prefix was replaced by a 'C'. In the end, those cars which were altered kept their original numbers and a small 'c' was added as a suffix.

The 88 extra compressors required were to be obtained through a swap. The KLL4 mounted on the trailer in a 4-car unit was to be removed and placed under the trailer of the 3-car unit. Its place was to be taken by a new compressor purchased from Westinghouse, who had developed a reciprocating compressor small enough to fit under a tube car (their type DHC2) and it was hoped that it would perform better than the KLL4.

When it was decided to uncouple 1938 stock on the Piccadilly, the stock allocation programme had to be revised yet again and the number of standard 3-car units available for the Northern Line off-peak service was reduced from 88 to 69. The compressors required were correspondingly reduced and thus money was saved. The new stock allocation now looked like this:

	Train End	
	'A'	'D'
Piccadilly:	4 + 3	trains: 15 x 7-cars (4-car west)
Bakerloo:	3 + 4	trains: 8 x 7-cars (4-car south)
	3U + 4	trains: 46 x 7-cars
Northern:	4 + 3	trains: 37 x 7-cars
	3 + 4	trains: 32 x 7-cars
	4 + 3U	trains: 46 x 7-cars

(U = 3-car unit with UNDM)
69 x 3-car units to have
2 compressors.

The UNDMs would not now run next to each other. The Bakerloo had 46 trains made up with one 'D' UNDM on the 3-car unit while the Northern had another 46 made up with an 'A' UNDM on the 3-car unit as follows:

Bakerloo:
'A' DM–T–'D' UNDM + 'A' DM–T–NDM–'D' DM
Northern:
'A' DM–T–NDM–'D' DM + 'A' UNDM–T–'D' DM

The block train concept had now virtually disappeared. On the Bakerloo in particular, the bulk of the uncoupling would be performed with trains containing UNDMs. It was therefore proposed that some form of driver's controls should be provided at the ends of UNDMs.

The concept of the UNDM arose, as we have seen, from the idea that some form of easy uncoupling was necessary in an emergency or for depot purposes. To apply the same easy uncoupling concept to running lines was, however, a different matter; although there was a precedent – the District Line. On that line uncoupling at a point in the train where there was only one driver's cab was commonplace; indeed, it was standard practice. It had also been applied to the new R stock, then being introduced, complete with automatic couplers. The system relied upon the detachment of a 2-car portion from the east end of the train. It had a cab at its east end but not at the west end. To reduce the length of the train, it was uncoupled at the autocoupler position and then the 2-cars driven away from the east end cab. To couple, the driver drove the 6-car portion up to the 2-car unit. This was always done at the east end of the train.

The R stock had uncoupling NDMs similar to the UNDMs proposed for the 1949 tube stock, but they were not called UNDMs. The only control available on these cars was the passenger emergency handle which provided an emergency brake at the non-driving end of a unit being propelled. A man stationed at this end called instructions to the driver in the cab at the other end.

This method of operation was not always possible on the tube lines. The District had special sidings available at uncoupling points and, as we have seen, it was always arranged to have the uncoupling unit at the east end of the train. Such provisions were impossible on the Northern for example; both the loop at Kennington and the intention to use 3-car units on the City branch precluded any idea of keeping uncoupling portions at particular ends of the trains. These problems made the operating department believe it essential to have some form of driving control at the non-driving end of the unit. From this need, the idea of the 'shunting control cabinet' was born.

The shunting control cabinet was originally conceived as a small cupboard let into the end bulkhead of the outer end of the UNDM car. It was to have a simple air brake valve and a motoring push button which would allow the unit to run up to series motoring. It was later developed to have air gauges, a whistle and head and tail light switches. It provided a considerable design headache at the time and was to delay the delivery of the new cars by several months.

Above left **The shunting control cabinet of an UNDM car. The large black button was the power control which gave 'shunt' or 'series' according to the position of the key operated switch to its left. Below, a brake valve of the Westinghouse No.6 type gave elementary air brake control.** LT Museum

Above Right **Many of the UNDM cars were converted from non-driving motor cars of 1938 stock. Here, car 92466 is in the process of conversion at Acton Works prior to its becoming 30021 in December 1952.** LT Museum

UNDM and driving motor coupled. Note that the UNDM car has no shoebeams. These cars were provided with a new type of beamless shoegear and shoe lifting equipment. After a few troubled years in service, they were provided with conventional shoegear. LUL

One of the main reasons for the operating demands was the intention to drive from the UNDM end of units on the running lines. All the usual safety devices – whistle, headlights, tripcock – were wanted. The only drawback was the need to provide a forward lookout for the driver whilst allowing him control of the train. This was difficult but it was done by allowing a push button motoring mode.

While construction of the new cars on order progressed and conversion work began at Acton on the streamlined cars, the government was coping with the economic crisis. In looking for ways of saving money, new projects were an easy target, particularly if construction hadn't started. The Camberwell extension was just such a project. It was cancelled in September 1950. There is no doubt that, were it not for the advanced state of construction of the 91 cars of 1949 tube stock, they would have been cancelled too. By this time though, it would have cost almost as much in penalties for cancelling as it would to continue. The first of the new cars was intended for delivery in the spring of 1951.

The Flat Ended Unit

Almost the only constant amongst all the 1949 programme alterations was the conversion of the streamlined 1935 stock cars to trailers and the dispatch of the flat-ended cars to the Central Line. The fate of the converted trailers we will see in due course but the flat-ended cars had an interesting story all of their own.

Late in 1949 work began on their conversion to operate as two-car shuttle units for the Central Line. The conversion of the six cars involved replacing the automatic couplers at the driving ends with the 'Ward'

mechanical type, this being in common with the pre-1938 tube stock then operating on the main Central Line. Also fitted were air hoses and passenger-open push buttons. The bogies on these six cars had not been modified to 1938 tube stock standard as they had not had an overhaul, so they were replaced with modified bogies from some of the streamlined motor cars. The MV electrical equipment was removed and replaced by the PCM type, which was obtained from 10003/7/8 and 11003/7/8. The guard's control positions were removed from the cabs and were relocated at the trailing end of the passenger saloon, but on the 'D' 11xxx cars only – the guard thus operated from one position, irrespective of whether this car was leading or trailing. The semi-permanent bar coupling was retained between cars. Compressors of the KLL4 type were fitted on all six motor cars, giving two compressors on each two-car unit.

Some of the destination blinds that needed replacement were taken out and never replaced, and destination plates from pre-1938 tube stock trains were often seen wedged in a prominent position, with the blind box left empty, although 10011 – 11011 appear to have retained blinds right up to the end. The use of the shuttle units was mainly confined to the Loughton-Epping shuttle and, to a lesser extent, the Hainault-Woodford shuttle. The conversion work was completed on all cars by August 1950 and the first two units entered service in October. The last followed in February 1951.

1935 stock at work on the Hainault-Woodford shuttle of the Central Line in the 1950s. J.A.S. Milne

On 17th May 1954, all three units returned to the Piccadilly Line for use on the Holborn-Aldwych shuttle service, but with the passenger door open control disconnected. Whilst in service on 3rd April 1955, driving motor 11010 was damaged in a collision with the stops beyond Aldwych station and much of the driving cab had to be rebuilt at Acton Works. Because of this rebuilding, it reappeared looking more like a 1938 tube stock car, in that the train number bracket was located in the front cab door and the side cab doors did not extend up into the curve of the roof.

Two of the units returned to the Central Line for the Epping-Ongar shuttle service (which commenced on 18th November 1957), 10009-11009 on 6th July 1957, and 10010-11010 on 20th August 1957. As two trains were then required for the Epping-Ongar shuttle and the third shuttle unit had been retained for test train duties, a third (spare) train was provided by borrowing a three-car train of 1938 tube stock from the Northern Line (10177-012265-11177). It was transferred on 16th November 1957 and returned to the Northern Line on 5th June 1960. This was the only 1938 stock train ever to run in service on the Central Line. This unit was able to operate on its own as a three-car train, having two compressors on the trailer.

The third shuttle unit (10011-11011) did not go back to the Central Line as it had been earmarked for some special trials with regenerative braking equipment. Regeneration, where the traction motors become generators during braking and feed current back into the supply system for use by other trains, had already been used on the Metadyne equipped O and P surface stocks since before the war, but the equipment had become unreliable and expensive to maintain. Moves had already begun to re-equip all the O and P stocks with PCM equipment and dispose of the Metadyne machines, but the hope persisted (and still does today) that regeneration could become a viable and reliable system.

Early in 1957 therefore, 10011-11011 unit was moved to Ealing Common Depot for preparation to receive a set of BTH regenerative braking equipment. The equipment was mounted inside the passenger saloons and the brake controllers were modified to take a mercury self-lapping switch which tilted as the driver moved the brake handle. Trial running on the Northfields to Acton Town test track, with the substation at Northfields specially modified to cope with regenerated current, began in May 1957. Early in 1958 the BTH equipment was replaced by GEC equipment for further trials and, finally, a Metropolitan-Vickers system was tested. Although regeneration was not adopted for new stock following these trials, many useful lessons were learned and the BTH equipment was cannibalised for trials with rheostatic braking systems first tried on a 1960 tube stock unit and later, after much modification, became the design basis for the rheostatic system first used on the Victoria Line's 1967 tube stock.

Meanwhile, it had been decided to increase the passenger accommodation on the Epping–Ongar line by lengthening the trains from two to three cars. This was achieved by converting three pre-1938 tube stock trailers of 1927 vintage, one to be formed in each shuttle unit. As both DMs of the shuttle units had compressors, these trailers were converted without compressors being fitted. They were converted between February and December 1958.

The regenerative test unit (10011-11011) was converted back to normal condition and given its converted trailer No. 70510 (which had been stored awaiting its parent cars' release from testing duties) in May 1960. The experimental self-lapping brake controllers with their tilting mercury switches were fitted to the rheostatic test unit of 1960 stock and one of them finally ended up in service on the District Line as a trial in an R stock cab.

When transferred back to the Central Line, the passenger-open door control was reinstated on units 10009-11009 and 10010-11010, and was also operative on converted trailers 70511 and 70512. However, by the time 10011-11011 re-entered service in May 1960 this facility had been withdrawn from all rolling stock, and converted trailer 70510 also had its passenger-open door control removed.

The cars retained their red livery until unpainted aluminium stock had taken over the main Central Line services. It was then decided that the shuttle units should be painted silver to match. This was done on the first unit in August 1963. The last unit was done in May 1965.

In 1964 the 1927 converted trailers were fitted with de-icing equipment, being confined to work on probably the most exposed section of the Central Line.

The silver repainting was done during their last overhaul, for their unreliability in service caused all three units to be stored out of service at Hainault from 7th December 1966. They were all eventually transferred to Ruislip, 10011-70510-11011 being the last to move. The shuttle service was taken over by 1962 stock, as used on the rest of the Central Line.

Late in 1968 plans for the replacement of the 1938 tube stock on the Bakerloo and Northern Lines were being formulated, the proposed new stock then being designated 1972 tube stock – and far different inconcept from the 1972 tube stock we know today.

It was proposed that the new trains would be eight cars of similar length to the seven cars they replaced, so that the train formation would be symmetrical. Each train would be formed into two four-car units, each having two cars of each unit formed back-to-back in articulated pairs. Consideration was also given to a conventional six-car train formation of two three-car units but this was abandoned because some station platforms were considered too sharply curved for the longer cars; similarly, nine-car block articulated trains of equivalent length was also an option, but this was abandoned because just one car with a defect would render the complete train out of service, rather than one unit as with the existing system.

For articulation trials, DMS 10010 and 11010 were transferred between pilot motor cars from Ruislip to Acton Works for preliminary tests on 1st November 1968 and 14th April 1969 respectively, and returned in August 1969 and May 1969 respectively, then being stored for scrap along with sister cars 10009 and 11009

and converted trailers 70511 and 70512. Unit 10011-70510-11011 was taken to Acton Works on 15th May 1969, where the two DMs were to become a test unit for articulated coupling between the trailing ends of the cars. The redundant trailer was taken back to Ruislip for scrap with the other cars.

For the articulation tests the cars were made shorter by cutting their trailing ends and mounting the trailing ends on one specially constructed bogie. Two new cast aluminium bogies of an unusual design, each with two new 1967 tube stock type traction motors, were fitted at the outer ends and 'metacone' air suspension was provided. The cars initially remained in painted silver livery and continued to carry their own numbers (10011-11011).

Extensive testing was carried out during the period 1970-72, including coupling the test unit with a four-car train of 1960 tube stock. Following on from these tests, a mock-up car was then proposed to be built at Acton Works. However, with the Heathrow extension

being authorised, attention immediately turned to providing new stock for the Piccadilly Line (the 1973 tube stock, for which the mock-up was already built), and transferring the 1959 stock to the Northern Line.

When the articulated train project was abandoned, the unit was transferred to the service stock fleet and was painted in service stock maroon in May 1972. It was then used as a shunting unit at Acton Works, being especially useful for bridging conductor rail gaps in the yard, and was numbered L14A and L14B (ex-10011 and 11011 respectively).

The other cars which were awaiting scrapping were cut up at Ruislip Depot, the official scrapping date being 10th October 1971. Cars L14A and L14B were withdrawn in February 1974 and were stored at Acton Works pending scrapping, latterly on accommodation bogies as the experimental bogies at the driving ends were used on 1972 MkII stock DM car 3363 for further testing purposes. The car bodies of L14A and L14B were cut up at Acton in February 1975.

Morden depot as remembered by many, with 1938 stock stabled neatly inside and outside on 29th May 1950. John H. Meredith

The 1949 Conversion

Apart from the purchase of the 91 new 1949 stock cars, there was a big programme of conversion work for the 1938 stock. This began early in 1950 with the start of work on rebuilding the 1935 streamlined motor cars to trailers. The first car was completed as No. 012484 in August 1950 and was put into service on the Northern Line the next month. It was carefully watched to see if the conversion had been a success and what modifications, if any, were necessary when converting the remaining 17 cars.

The work involved was quite extensive. Aside from cutting away the streamlined cab end rebuilding it as a trailer end, the traction equipment had to be removed and the car completely rewired. A compressor was fitted and the cars provided with passenger door control. The finished job gave them a typical 1938 type look but there were obvious differences. There were only three windows on each side of the end bays instead of four and there was more room between the single end doorway and the car end. There were some modifications which appeared on the remaining 17 cars as a result of running experience with 012484, mainly concerning doors and bogies. While this was going on a detailed programme had been drawn up for the conversion of existing 1938 cars and the delivery of the 1949 stock.

Most of the conversion work concerned the nine cars of block train stock which had to be standardised or altered. They were to be dealt with in stages. The first stage was to use newly-converted 1935 stock trailer

cars to replace the special NDM cars in the six type I block trains running on the Northern Line. At the same time some standardisation was to be done to other cars in these trains. They were reformed as follows:

Position: 1 '35' 2   7   (8)   9
Car: DM− T − NDM−T− SNDM× NDM− DM

Compare this formation with that on page 61. The 1935 trailer replaced the No.2 NDM which moved to the No.3 SNDM spot. The No.2 NDM was standardised and had its Ward coupler removed. The No.(8) NDM was also partially standardised at this time. It had new motors and shoegear fitted and its traction control equipment was given a special overhaul. However, it retained its Ward coupler. In addition, the DMs had the guards controls fitted at the usual position. All this work was done at Morden Depot and the six trains were completed by April 1951. The 6 SNDMs left were removed and sent to Acton for storage pending the arrival of equipment for their conversion.

The next stage in the programme was the conversion of SNDMs to UNDMs. The prototype conversion, car No.92461, was sent to Acton early in 1951, after removal from the first of the block trains mentioned above, and was completed at the end of April. Although the other SNDMs released by Morden were already at Acton by that time, no more work could be done until the autocouplers and shunting control cabinets were delivered. There was a considerable delay with this and the first converted car, as No. 30015, was not shown to operating staff representatives until early in December 1951. Staff training commenced in January 1952 and the first passenger carrying block train with UNDMs in it ran on the Northern Line in

The southern terminus of the Northern Line at Morden in the late 1960s. The Edgware train seen entering the tunnel would not see daylight until just south of Golders Green.
R.J. Greenaway Collection

February 1952. However, it ran without the UNDM shunting controls fitted.

The block train method of operation was continued for a time using the new UNDMs. They were placed in the middle of a reformed type I block train thus:

Position: 1   '35'   2   'D'   'A'   9
Car: DM− T −NDM− UNDM+ UNDM−T− DM

The DM in position 1, the '35' stock converted trailer, the No.2 NDM and the No.9 DM all remained in the same positions. The two UNDMs went in the middle and the trailer displaced by the 'D' UNDM was moved next to the No.9 DM. Most of the DMs were renumbered into the 1xxxx series at the time but some retained their 9xxxx numbers for a few months after UNDMs were incorporated into their trains. The 'D' UNDM used in these formations was a new car from the 91 ordered, the first being delivered from Birmingham in November 1951. Between February and July 1952 the number of block trains which entered service with two UNDMs rose to 11, all on the Northern. Some of them had been formed from 3-car standard units by placing two UNDMs, a trailer and an NDM in between the existing cars. Six other units had also been formed with a 3-car DM-T-UNDM formation and a further five of these went into service on the Bakerloo from September 1952. The Northern eventually had 14 block trains with two UNDMs, many without shunting controls.

The Piccadilly Line was programmed to receive 15 x 7-cars of standard 4 + 3 car formation 1938 stock. The first of these was transferred to Northfields Depot in February 1952 for training and a second was sent over in May. The Piccadilly had already seen some 1938 stock as some preliminary test units and gauging runs had taken place at various times since June 1950. The first passenger carrying trains entered service as a fleet of five trains which were introduced with the new winter timetable in September 1952. By this time, however, a new development had taken place.

In June 1952, the trainmen's union representatives suddenly refused to use UNDMs for uncoupling at Watford. They said that for the long trip of three miles from Watford Junction to Croxley Green Depot the UNDM driving position was inadequate, particularly as there was no deadman handle and no proper lookout window. In the pouring rain and with no window wiper it might be said they had a point. As it was intended to have 46 x 3-car unit with 'D' UNDMs at the south end for uncoupling purposes on the Bakerloo, this ultimatum came as a nasty surprise. A hasty reappraisal of the programme was done.

After a good deal of discussion over the next few weeks a relatively simple solution was found. It was decided to swap 15 x 3-car two-DM units intended for the Piccadilly with 15 x 3-car UNDM units on the Bakerloo and make sure when allocating trains for service that UNDMs did not have to be used at Watford. The stock position was now to be as follows:

Piccadilly:	15 x 7-cars of 3U + 4 cars
Bakerloo:	31 x 7-cars of 3U + 4 cars
	23 x 7-cars of 3 + 4 cars
Northern:	No change.

Because of this the Piccadilly began getting UNDMs in October 1952 and they were inserted into existing trains and run only during the peaks as block trains while crews were given training in the use of UNDMs. The original intention to allow the 1938 trains on the Piccadilly to run on uncoupling turns was not abandoned at this time but the introduction of UNDMs served to delay the implementation while crews were trained and because of a further problem. This concerned the train formation on the Piccadilly; the uncoupling portions on the 1938 trains were now all at the wrong end. It was the practice to uncouple trains on the Piccadilly from the east end and all the Standard stock trains were formed with the 3-car portion at that end. It was intended that the 1938 stock should be worked in the same way and indeed, trains were originally formed up that way. Once it became known that the UNDMs were to replace the 'D' DMs on the 3-car units, of course they had to be formed with the 3-car at the west end thus:

Planned:
'A' DM-T-NDM-'D' DM + 'A' DM-T-'D' DM
Actual:
'A' DM-T-'D' UNDM + 'A' DM-T-NDM-'D' DM

It was a simple task involving uncoupling the 3-car and recoupling it at the other end.

The alteration had the effect of making the 1938 stock a 3U + 4 car formation while the rest of the stock on the line was 4 + 3U car. It was very restrictive operationally because it prevented the use of these trains on uncoupling turns and so, to get over this problem, the 1938 stock was turned wrong way round. Each train was sent on a turning trip via Earl's Court (District) to High Street Kensington (reverse), South

Kensington (reverse) and then back to the Piccadilly Line. All were done in time for their introduction to uncoupling on 2nd February 1953. They were however, required to be right-way round for overhaul at Acton and every time one was sent there it had to be turned again. This situation remained until early in 1961 when uncoupling on the tube lines was permanently cancelled and the trains then reverted to their normal direction.

By the spring of 1953 the 1949 programme was well advanced. All 91 new cars had been delivered and the bulk of the conversion work was complete. Because of delays in equipment delivery, however, many of the new cars were delivered to Ruislip, transferred to Ealing Common for commissioning and the fitting of motors and then sent to Hammersmith for storage. At one time there were 18 cars stored there. There were further delays because of collision damage sustained in depots. There were nine DMs and two trailers in Acton for repairs in February 1953 in addition to the last two SNDMs being converted to UNDMs.

The collisions were not really a result of a fall in driving standards so much as a reflection of how much was being done in reforming trains during this period. The number of 1938/49 stock cars involved in unit reformations was over 450 and transfer moves between lines totalled 330, excluding new stock arrivals and moves to and from Acton and Hammersmith. No wonder there were some collisions.

At this time there were still 8 trains on the Northern with two UNDMs in their formation and some of these remained until repairs on the damaged cars were completed later in the year. Once this was done the planned reformations were carried out and the stock settled down to a relatively uneventful period of 15 years during which time little changed.

Chapter 5
Design Changes and Experiments

Experience with the 1938 stock had shown that there were a number of substantial improvements which could be made on new cars without rendering them incapable of working with the existing stock. When the 1949 tube stock was ordered therefore, these were incorporated into the design.

The most obvious improvement was in the bogie. The all-welded 1938 design had proved very troublesome. The principal disadvantage was in the stiffness of the frame. Stresses were set up during running which caused cracks and a considerable amount of repair work was necessary. For the 1949 bogie, a new design was produced which involved riveting the cross members to the side frames, thus allowing some flexing in the structure. At the same time, the bolster design was revised so that the springs were outside the bogie solebars and the bay formation of the 1938 design was dispensed with.

Another new feature of the 1949 bogie was the shoegear. Traditionally this had always been hung from a wooden beam attached, for the positive shoe at least, between the axleboxes. For the 1949 design, the beam was dispensed with and special shoe lifting gear provided. It was very similar to the design produced for the District Line's R stock. Like the R stock design it soon ran into trouble and it was replaced with the traditional shoebeam system in 1960-61.

The PCM traction control equipment was also modified. An extra pair of cam contactors was inserted on the camshaft to reduce contact damage and a new type of lightweight resistor grid was adopted. There were also modifications to the volt and current detection system, which had been by separate low current and no-volt relays on the 1938 stock. They were combined to form a volt-amp relay on the 1949 equipment.

Door controls were also improved. The pre-war use of passenger door control, stopped for the duration, was reinstated with the improved system first tried on a 1938 train on the Northern Line in 1940. All trains were eventually converted to the same system and PDC was re-introduced on the Bakerloo in December 1949 and on the Northern in April 1950. When the 1949 stock was introduced it had PDC, of course, but it had a new type of door interlock known as the mercury type. Instead of relying on metal to metal contacts, the

new, tilting interlock used the current conducting properties of mercury to complete the round-the-train door circuit. Although it gave much trouble in the early years of its use, it was gradually improved and eventually became an LT standard type.

There were other minor technical improvements introduced with the 1949 stock, including a revised e.p. brake circuit intended to overcome electrical problems with the retarder control system. Eventually too, the feed valves provided on each car to restrict the air supply to the e.p. brake equipment were removed from all 1938 type trains. They had been provided on early e.p. brake fitted trains to prevent excessive air pressure causing over-braking and flatted wheels. They were retained when self-lapping and retarder controlled brakes were introduced but they were really unnecessary. However, natural caution and the fear of increasing the incidence of flatted wheels meant that they were retained on 1938 and 1949 cars until a programme for their removal was begun in 1953 after a series of lengthy tests.

Of course the UNDMs were the most innovative of the 1949 vehicles. The shunting control cabinet with which they were fitted, once it had been perfected, proved a useful system and survived the stock to which it was originally fitted. When the UNDMs were withdrawn in the early 1970s the cabinets were saved and fitted to new 1972 stock UNDMs.

It is sad to reflect that, in the midst of this regeneration of the 1938 stock and the concurrent delivery of the District Line's R stock, W.S. Graff-Baker died suddenly. He collapsed in the street outside his home in Kensington, in February 1952. With his passing, an era ended. At no time, before or since his reign as Chief Mechanical Engineer of the London Underground, was so much technical innovation introduced. Even as the 1949 design work was progressing, plans were being drawn up for a new tube stock, the 1952 stock. Amongst other things, Graff-Baker intended that this stock would have dual control circuits supplying alternate cars along the train. This was proposed early in 1950. The 1952 stock did not appear until much later, by which time it had become the 1959 stock and, by then, innovation had long been dead. The 1959 stock was an aluminium-bodied copy of the 1938 stock with minor improvements. The dual control circuit idea had to wait until the 1973 stock to see its adoption in the its originally intended form.

Another advanced idea which Graff-Baker suggested was the forward-and-aft controller. This was first tried on 1938 DM car 10221 in 1951 and consisted of a combined controller and brake handle with an under-mounted deadman grip. It was a good idea which was lost when he died and did not reappear in London until the introduction of the D78 stock in 1980, almost 30 years later.

The Numbering System

As mentioned earlier the 1935 experimental tube stock saw the introduction of a new system for car numbering on the tube lines which involved the use of five or six figure numbers. The same system was continued for the 1938 and 1949 stocks as follows:

No. Series	Type of Car
10xxx	'A' Driving Motor
11xxx	'D' Driving Motor
12xxx	Non- Driving Motor
012xxx	Trailer
90xxx	'A' Driving Motor (9-car trains)
91xxx	'D' Driving Motor (9-car trains)
920xx	Non-Driving Motor (9-car trains)
924xx	Special Non-Driving Motor (9-car trains)
092xxx	Trailer (9-car trains)
A92xxx	Trailer (Standardised for Bakerloo)
30xxx	'A' Uncoupling Non-Driving Motor
31xxx	'D' Uncoupling Non-Driving Motor
012xxxC	Trailer (with two compressors)
705xx	58 Trailer (1927 converted stock)

It was originally planned that all the new trains would be composed of all motor cars, and that all units would be of two cars. A 2-car unit would have a numerically matching pair of cars, e.g. 10012-11012. When 3-car units were introduced into the plan, it was still intended to retain all-motor-car trains. The extra car would be numbered in the 12000 series and units made up thus: 10012-12012-11012. With the realisation that all motor-car trains would be too powerful for the current supply and too fast for the signalling system, and the consequent introduction of trailers, the 012xxx series of numbers was introduced. It was hoped that all-motor-cars would eventually be the rule and that all trailers would become NDMs. Renumbering them was then simply a matter of removing the leading zero.

Although the matching number concept could have been applied to the trailer units thus: 10158-012158-11158 or (in the case of 58 trailers) 10013-70513-11013, it was abandoned soon after the decision to use converted 1927 cars and could never really have survived with all the renumbering and reforming which went on during the late 1930s. However, the idea of retaining the matching motor-car pairs survived until the final days of the stock. It was only abandoned when UNDMs were introduced or when units were temporarily reformed because of programme changes or collision repairs.

A renewed attempt to get like units into blocks of numbers occurred during the 1949 uncoupling programme. The 3-car units which were fitted with two compressors were arranged in a consecutive series of numbers: 10151-012xxxC-11151 to 10287-012xxxC-11287 odd numbers only. The whole stock was allocated as follows:

10012 to 10040 (evens)	4-car units on Piccadilly
10013 to 10041 (odds)	3-cars with 31xxx UNDMs on Piccadilly
10042 to 10148 (evens)	4-car units on Bakerloo
10043 to 10103 (odds)	3-cars with 31xxx UNDMs on Bakerloo
10105 to 10149 (odds)	3-car units on Bakerloo
10151 to 10287 (odds)	3-cars with 2 compressors on Northern
10150 to 10288 (evens)	4-car units on Northern
11013 to 11101 (odds)	3-cars with 30xxx UNDMs on Northern
10289 to 10333	4-car units on Northern

This was the eventual allocation of the stock. However, transfers took place from time to time and, over the years up to 1970, some 10 cars were withdrawn, mostly as a result of accidents, and a number of units were reformed.

The 1949 programme saw a lot of renumbering. All the 90xxx and 91xxx driving motor cars were renumbered into the 10xxx and 11xxx series but not necessarily at the time they were standardised. The 924xx SNDMs were all renumbered into the 30xxx series upon their conversion to UNDMs. Two 120xx cars also became 30xxx UNDMs. The other 9-car train vehicles were given standard numbers as they were formed into standard units, merely by changing the '9' digit for a '1'.

The introduction of a system based on five-digit car numbers had been firmly resisted by the many traditionalists on the Underground when it was first proposed in 1935. There would be an increase in recording errors, it was said, and the great variety of numbering and renumbering was causing enough headaches already. Graff-Baker countered the opposition by pushing the matching pairs idea. It was a pity it never survived in its original form but the principle was retained and refined and has survived to this day.

Tests and Modifications

Over the years, many 1938 stock cars were used as test beds for various modifications and for trials of new equipment. Some began during the war, including the first trial of a train set of tilting mercury door interlocks which entered service on the Northern Line in April 1942. There were also tests with brake blocks.

Traditionally, all Underground trains had cast iron brake blocks. They were cheap and effective but they were very hard on wheel wear, they produced an inflammable dust and they could cause flaking of rail heads at some critical places. For many years attempts had been made to get rid of them, with varying success. They had been replaced by non-metallic blocks on stock used solely in tunnel sections but once the long

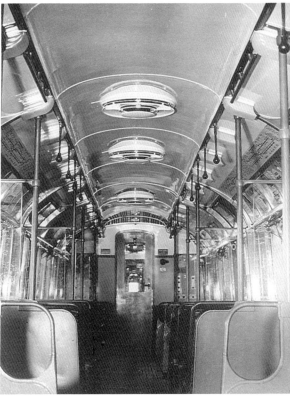

Above Left **Originally, the interiors of tube cars had the maps positioned over the advertisements which were above the windows. This mock-up was to see the effect of placing the maps down the centre of the ceiling. It was done in April 1943 but probably never ran in service like this.** LT Museum

Above Right **A train of 1938 stock was experimentally fitted with ventilation fans in 1949. This photograph shows the installation provided for some of the cars by J. Stone. The idea was not adopted at that time.** LT Museum

extensions into the open came into use problems arose in wet weather. This was one of the principal reasons why the Bakerloo kept two separate groups of stock for many years.

When the 1938 stock was introduced it had cast iron blocks. Very soon however, non-metallic inserts were fitted into cast iron shells on a number of test trains. The cast iron shells were retained to act as a brake block guide as they had grooves to fit over the wheel flanges. Experiments with various types of inserts continued over the next few years until it was suggested that, with suitable guiding on the bogie, the block could be used on its own and the shell could be dispensed with. This was first tried on the Northern early in 1947. By the late 1950s all the more modern stocks had been converted and it eventually became a standard system on the Underground.

A less technical trial was carried out on at least one car in about 1943. A photograph survives showing a car with its line maps mounted along the centre of the ceiling. Another experiment involved a line map framed in bronze. Both these trials seem to have been connected with a subsequent change to the positions of maps and interior advertisements. Originally, cars entered service with the advertisements placed immediately above the side windows. Maps were above the advertisements. Sometime after the Second World War, the positions were reversed.

Another trial was carried out on car 10158 from April 1946. This involved replacing the original rubber handgrips with plastic ones. The rubber ones had been easy to remove and, it was suggested, could be used as weapons! There was even a story that one had been found in a street in North Africa! Plastic soon became the standard.

Although fans had been tried and then abandoned on the first 1935 experimental unit, 10000-11000, the hope that a tube car could be made quieter by closing the toplights and installing forced ventilation still persisted. In 1947 car 10320 had ceiling fans fitted which proved sufficiently encouraging for further trials. In November 1949 a train had various fan systems fitted as follows:

10138	)	GEC: 8 fans per car (600 volts)
012168	)	
12117	)	Patent Lighting Co: 8 per car (600v)
11318	)	
10023	)	
012173	)	J. Stone & Co: 12 per car (50v)
11023	)	

The same train had a system of door fault indicator lights fitted. The fans were not considered worth adopting as standard and they were removed by April 1952, but the door fault lights were considered a good idea and trials with them continued. At first they were mounted behind a flat glass disc fitted onto the car roof. This was very difficult to see from the guard's position at the end of the train so the design was changed to allow a small glass dome to protrude from the roof. This solved the visibility problem and it eventually became a standard design, first appearing on the 1956 tube stock. It was removed from the 1938 stock test train in the 1950s.

On the standard interior fittings of 1938 and contemporary surface stock was the fluted glass lamp shades. Unfortunately, they broke easily and were very expensive to replace. Cars 11299 and 012347 were fitted with plastic shades in November 1948 and ran with them until September 1952. They were not adopted however and eventually all the shades were removed in 1959. Over the years a number of trials were carried out on 1938 cars to test new types of control equipment. In December 1947, cars 10202 and 11202 entered service with an improved version of the PCM equipment which was intended for the R and 1949 stocks. In February 1948, car 10230 had a desk type master controller fitted. This was a new attempt to give the driver a better working position and was adopted for the R and subsequent stocks. In September 1950, and R stock type fluid speedometer was installed on car 10210.

In October 1954 a trial GEC designed camshaft was tried on 10200 on the Northern and a further version of it went under 10026 on the Piccadilly Line from December 1956. The big order for new stock which was expected in the late fifties alerted GEC to the possibilities of an order with LT. Their equipment never became a replacement for the BTH PCM system even when they took over the BTH company in 1960. Neither did another rival, English Electric, who had their equipment fitted on car 10178 on the Northern during 1958.

BTH also tried out a new traction control system as a prototype for 4-motor control intended for the 1960 and A60 stocks. This was the PCU system which was first tried on 12132 in May 1956 and then in a revised form on cars 10228 and 10326 from January 1959. Although 4-motor control was adopted, the PCU system did not find favour.

Top In 1951, car 10230 had this experimental forward-and-aft controller fitted. It operated both power and e.p. brakes. It was not adopted then but was to appear in a revised form on the District Line's D78 stock. BTH

Right In an attempt to overcome the nuisance of passengers blocking doorways, large standback spaces and perch seats were experimentally fitted to 1938 trailer 012339 in 1956. They remained on the car until it was scrapped in 1977. LT Museum

More visible experiments were also tried out on various cars. Fluorescent lighting was provided in 11294 from November 1953 and survived until January 1959. Car 012339 had a revised seating arrangement near one of its double doorways. A set of 'perch seats' was fitted so that standing passengers could partially rest on them and it opened up a much wider standing area near the doors where it was most needed. It was really the forerunner of the standback space first provided next to the doors on the 1960 and subsequent stock. The experiment first saw passengers in January 1956.

Various revised decor schemes were tried on 1938 cars. R stock type moquette for seats was first tried on car 11016 in August 1948. It was then put into service on the Bakerloo in a block train. In October 1955 the interiors of 12006 and 11024 were repainted in a pale blue/grey finish as a prototype for the 1956 tube stock. The seats were upholstered in a new moquette at the same time and remained with it until July 1967.

One of the innovations for the 1956/59/62 series of tube stocks was the use of rubber suspension. Trials had been carried out for many years beforehand and a number of these were done on 1938 cars. The object was to allow rubber to replace steel in the major suspension components in a drive to eliminate a critical source of wear and failure. Trials began early in 1953 when car 31016 was fitted with Metalstik rubber bolster suspension and were continued on 11141, which had a complete set of rubber suspension fitted early in 1954. It was exhibited at the May 1954 International Railway Convention exhibition at Willesden and then went into service on the Bakerloo in July. It was transferred to the Piccadilly in November 1954. Another car was fitted with Spencer Moulton suspension in 1956. This was car number 012495, which was also sent to the Piccadilly Line from the Northern specially for the trials. Many tests were carried out on the Piccadilly in preference to other lines when possible because of the availability of the test tracks between Acton Town and Northfields and because the depot at Northfields was close to Acton where the design offices were located.

Both 11141 and 012495 were used for other tests on the Piccadilly Line. Number 11141 had a new design of driver's brake valve fitted. It incorporated the use of poppet valves instead of the faceplate valves traditionally used. In its experimental form it required a special key which had to be collected by the driver from the depot office whenever he had to drive from this car. Number 012495 had a less obvious modification in the form of a single door valve. This opened all the doors on one side of the car and replaced the individual valves provided for each door leaf. It was adopted as a standard design for future stocks once it was decided, in 1959, to abandon passenger door control on all lines.

Perhaps the best known trial carried out on a 1938 stock car is the bodywork conversion of 10306 in the summer of 1949. This car, variously known as 'the high window car', 'the vista car' or 'the sunshine window car' was fitted with special windows and doors. It was chosen because it happened to be in the works at the time.

Prior to the work being done on 10306, another car (11237) which was in the works for repairs following collision damage, had a partial conversion of the body to see how it would look. The Chairman saw it on 13th May 1949 and approved the full conversion of a complete car. The experiment was part of the early design work being carried out for future tube stock. It was hoped to introduce it on what was then called the 1951 (later 1952) tube stock. Graff-Baker had the idea that it was inconvenient for standing passengers to have to stoop to see the names of stations. To help them he proposed extending the windows up into the roof. The central pairs of windows between the doors were done as were the doors themselves. The door pocket windows were replaced by circular windows.

Car 012495 was used to test a number of new systems. One was the Spencer Moulton bogie, seen at Acton Works in 1957. LUL

The car was completed in November 1949 and, after some modifications to the glazing to improve the waterproofing and to allow easier changing of the glass, it was sent to Neasden in February 1950 and entered service on the Bakerloo early in that month. In March 1951 it went to the Northern as part of the 1949 programme and stayed there until it was withdrawn early in 1978 for use as part of a pilot unit working with a 1973 stock experimental tube train (ETT).

It is interesting to note that it was decided to abandon the idea of high windows in new cars because it was more expensive than the conventional design. At the same time it was suggested that perhaps only the doors should be done. This was also dismissed because, although the increased cost was marginal, it was considered it would 'spoil the appearance of the side elevation'. It eventually came to tube cars on the 1967 stock.

Left In November 1949, work was completed on the conversion of car 10306 to a special window design. The door and some of the window glazing was extended up into the roof in an attempt to help standing passengers to see the station names. The car is seen at Acton Works immediately after conversion. LT Museum

Below The interior of 10306. LT Museum

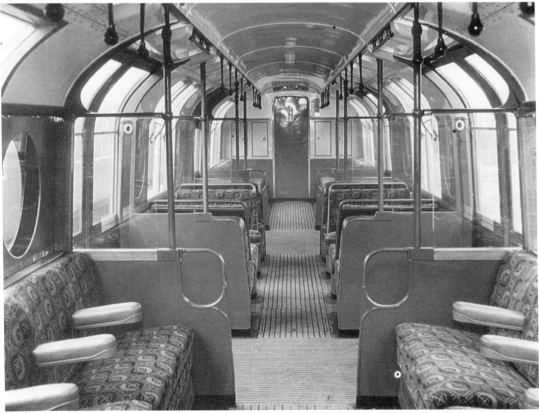

Above **The prototype conversion carried out at Acton on part of car 11237 in May 1949.** H. Clarke/LURS

Right **Detail of the conversion of 10306. Note the differences between this and the work done on 11237.** LT Museum

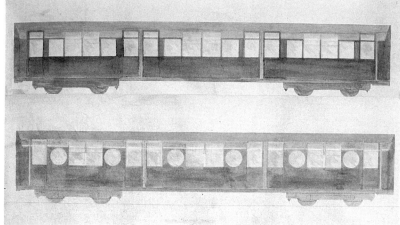

Drawings of two possible designs for the planned 1952 tube stock, clearly showing the 1938 stock ancestry. LUL

Interior of a mock-up produced at Acton Works of the planned 1952 stock design, incorporating some of the features of 10306 but with fluorescent lighting and ceiling fans. LUL

Chapter 6
The Intermediate Years

It is a widely recognised truth that railway rolling stock goes through three stages of life. The first stage is the time from the delivery of the first vehicle until the teething troubles are found and the trains go through a shakedown period. The next stage is the middle period when the stock settles down to a more or less uneventful life of useful, revenue earning service and when failure rates are low and modifications are few. This is the period at the bottom of the 'bathtub' named after the curve described by the failure rate of a rolling stock during its lifetime. Failure rates are high early in the life cycle whilst the bugs are taken care of, they then fall to a low level for a number of years and finally, they sharply rise to a higher level which usually marks the beginning of the end of the stock's useful life. This rise in the failure rate marks the third period.

For the 1938 tube stock, the life cycle clearly followed this pattern, although the change from the first period to the second was delayed by the war, the huge number of modifications required and by the introduction of the 1949 stock. It did not really begin its second stage of life until 1953 when all the reorganisation following the delivery of the 1949 cars was complete. There then followed a period of stability and reliability which lasted for 15 years until the sharp rise in failures in 1968 which was later aggravated by the industrial troubles at Acton Works.

This was also the period when A.W. Manser was in charge at Acton. He had taken over as CME from Graff-Baker upon the latter's untimely death in February 1952. His was a reign of solidity. Reliability was the watchword. Nothing new was done without an enormous amount of research and soul searching. His experience as engineer in charge of the Northern Line during the introduction of the 1938 stock had taught him the effects on service reliability of introducing radical designs into rolling stock. Most of the new ideas which came during this time were originally started in Graff-Baker's day – rubber suspension and aluminium bodies on tube cars for example – and only the Automatic Train Operation system can truly be said to have been begun in Manser's time.

Some experiments carried out on the 1938 stock during this period have already been mentioned – mostly trials of new versions of existing equipment.

Much thought was being given to the question of replacing the older Standard tube stock during the mid-1950s and one suggestion for the Central Line proposed the use of 1931 trailers, rehabilitated and painted silver, and coupled into units with new aluminium-bodied motor cars. As there were not enough 1931 trailers for the whole line, it was suggested that some 1927 trailers could be rebuilt with end doors to match the 1931 cars and so make up the number of units required. To test the idea a 58 trailer from the Bakerloo (70518) was rebuilt at Acton with end doors early in 1957. It re-entered service in June 1957. To test a cheaper method of reconstruction, a second car (70545) was done later in the year and re-entered service in January 1958. Although it was considered a practical scheme and the idea of running converted trailers with new motor cars was kept alive for the next few years, trains comprising all new cars were eventually ordered for the Central Line.

At Work with 1938 Stock

Once the 1938 stock had settled down following the completion of the 1949 uncoupling programme in 1953, there was the 15 year period between 1953 and 1968 when it can be said to have had its heyday. The Northern and Bakerloo were fully equipped with it and the Piccadilly Line had 15 x 7-car trains of it. It had become well known to Londoners and was fully understood by the operators and maintainers, something which had taken a long time to achieve, partly because of the war and partly because of the introduction of the UNDM concept with the 1949 stock. Apart from one or two continuing problems with MGs and compressors, the equipment worked well by the standards of the day and its performance was adequate, if not exactly outstanding. In spite of this, the stock was never well liked by the staff.

The operating managers were pleased at the increased carrying capacity of the new stock over the Standard stock but the crews were not so fond of them and the maintenance staff actively disliked them. Of course, the Standard stock had the distinct maintenance advantage that all its major equipment was 'upstairs', above the floor and easily accessible. The 1938 equipment was mostly under the floor and not so easily got at. It also had equipment cases at the sides, very close to the rail level, which led to side pits being provided in depots, where previously only centre pits were provided.

The maintenance aspects were not helped by the compact features. It was difficult to change brake blocks on motored axles because the motor got in the way. Brushes on compressor motors were difficult to get at because they were a tight fit and e.p. brake valves were difficult to refit because they were wired through holes in the pipe block. Much of the PCM equipment was also difficult to get at compared with Standard stock equipment because it was packed into underfloor cases and, as mentioned earlier, damage to compressor pipework was common when refitting them into the restricted space under cars.

Automatic couplers were a constant source of trouble. They often became gummed up with a sludge which choked the valves and caused sluggish operation. The electrics of these couplers demanded that both operated together in order to uncouple the units. Sluggish operation by either coupler meant that the units failed to uncouple. What then resulted was that what should have been a one-man job developed into a sort of joint operations/maintenance committee meeting. The crew involved in the uncoupling operation would first try to get both couplers to operate together by manually operating the valves located behind a seat in the driving cars. One of them would call out 'One, two three, Go!' and they would try to lift the valves together. A third man in the cab would be ready to back off the unit as soon as he felt the couplers part. If this method failed after several goes, it was time to get the 'fitters' involved.

The 'fitters', as the crews always called the maintenance staff, regardless of their grade or status, had two methods for freeing jammed couplers. One involved draining all the air out of both couplers and inserting a pin into a slot located in the top of the wedge piston on one coupler and levering it back to release the wedge. This was usually effective and allowed the other unit to be reversed away. The 'Guard Only' barrier bar, normally used to keep passengers clear of the guard's position, made an ideal lever.

The other method sometimes resorted to in the most stubborn cases was to reverse the air connections to the coupler. This meant that when the air pressure was restored, the wedges were permanently pushed back to the uncouple position. That would normally do the trick.

The automatic couplers were really too complex. There were a great many problems with them in the early days including a tendency to turn to the uncoupled position in the middle of the train. Usually only one of the two did this and the design was such that the units remained coupled but there was an emergency brake application, an audible warning in the cab to tell the driver that the e.p. brake had failed (it was actually only the interlock circuit across the coupler being opened) and the pilot light for the door circuit was lost. With all this happening at once, it was not surprising that the crew often became very confused and some long delays resulted. The problem was eventually solved with a minor modification to the operating valve but the incidents got the stock a bad name for being over-complicated.

The problems caused by sludge in the air system were numerous. Brake valves, door valves and couplers were all affected by it. It arose from a mixture of water and oil which collected in the pipes. The water was formed by condensation arising after compression, when the air was warmed, as it passed down the train and cooled. The oil was from lubricants. So much sludge was formed that it was necessary to drain the air system every 5-daily (later 7-daily) inspection. All trains suffered from it but the 1938 stock was particularly sensitive to it. So much water could be drained from a train that some depots kept a 40-gallon oil drum mounted on wheels which they could run under a train during draining.

There were a number of things the crews did not like about the 1938 stock. The door control system on the first trains to enter service incorporated passenger door control and on some there were the alterations caused by the modified 9-car train system used on the block trains. With the technical problems which followed their entry into service, these variations served only to confuse the guards who naturally preferred what they understood – the Standard stock system. Standard stock also had the advantage that the guard's position was well secluded, being almost a separate compartment from the passenger saloon on the pre-1931 stocks. The glazed draught screen of the 1938 stock left the guard in full view of the public, something he did not always relish when he wanted a smoke. Crews were, of course, forbidden to smoke on duty.

Drivers did not like the driving position. It was cramped compared with older stock and it was colder. Being close to all the electrical resistors, the Standard stock cab was warmer than the 1938 cab which only had one small heater in the wall behind the driver. In an attempt to warm the cab quickly some drivers would open the cab side door after entering the tunnel on the first early morning trip. Having stood all night in the open, even with its heaters on, the interior of a train gets very cold. It was much warmer in the tunnels, particularly south of Camden Town, and leaving the cab door open helped to dry out the damp and cold in the cab.

Draughts in cabs were (and still are) a constant problem and in this respect the 1938 stock was no better and no worse than other stocks. Moquette strips were originally provided on the cab door edges but they were not very effective and during the late 1960s nylon brush strips replaced them. It was a nice try but it could not stop the persistent problems in the corners or around the hinges.

At the other end of the temperature range, the cabs became very warm and stuffy in the summer. To help overcome this the cab ceiling had a 'Norvent' air ventilator fitted. To supplement the largely ineffective air supply thus provided, some drivers ran with the offside cab door open, even in the tunnel. This helped provide a draught but made for a lot more noise and dust.

Like any particular type of rolling stock, the 1938

stock had its peculiarities. Some of those well remembered are the soft suspension, the apparently slugged start, the awkward communicating door handles and the often sticky brake handle operation. The suspension came into its own on the Piccadilly Line over the non-stop section between Hammersmith and Acton Town. Here trains bounced and bucked their way along, not as ferociously as the 1959 stock, more like a ship in a rough sea. The Bakerloo between Neasden and Wembley Park also provided some lively riding, as did the Northern Line between High Barnet and Totteridge (southbound).

The slugged start was more apparent than real. The two Line Breakers were arranged so that the second only closed after the first, not at the same time. The result was that when the driver moved the controller to a motoring position there was a distinct 'clonk' as LB 1 closed, followed by the start of the motors as LB 2 closed.

The communicating door handles were a nuisance. The outside handle was a reasonably sized lever which allowed the door to be opened easily, although a sharp kick was often necessary because they tended to stick. But for some reason, the inside handle was a short stubby knob which seems to have been designed to remove skin from knuckles rather than open doors. The reason for this peculiarity is obscure.

Brakes were more important. As any driver will testify, it is embarrassing but not critical if a train will not start. If a train will not stop however, it is very critical. Of course, trains do not 'fail to stop', they have the emergency braking system which is always available. They can, however, have a tendency to stop in the wrong place and this is important on a line, like the Northern or Piccadilly, where a 7-car train has to be stopped in a platform designed for 6-car trains. Drivers therefore tend to be very critical of train braking.

The 1938 tube stock saw the first mass production self-lapping brake used in London. As a pioneer it led the way to better systems later on but it suffered to some extent because it was a first attempt. The old non-self-lapping system required the driver to move the brake handle twice for every adjustment in the braking force. The self-lapping system needed only one movement. It relied on a system of links attached to the brake handle shaft and to a piston which monitored the air pressure in the brake cylinders and attempted to match it relative to the position of the handle. Often this mechanism would attempt to drag the handle away from the brake application position chosen by the driver towards the release position. To prevent this the driver had to hold on to the handle all through the braking sequence.

Incidents of day-to-day operations come to mind. On

An accident at High Barnet where a train overran the shunting neck on 7th August 1953. The leading car has been supported by a stack of sleepers to prevent it rolling down into the street. LUL

one occasion a driver struggled to prevent his train overshooting the platform at almost every station. The braking rate available seemed to be lower than normal. His investigations led him to examine the two mercury retarders mounted in the cab. It later transpired that they had been incorrectly set thus giving a lower than standard braking rate.

On another occasion a train kept getting stuck with its brakes full on. It would only release if the driver 'notched up' i.e. jerked the power on and off in a manner often used to free a sticky door. The fault only appeared intermittently – as such gremlins are often wont to do – and could not be traced when the train was returned to depot after it had shut down the westbound Piccadilly Line at Acton Town for 25 minutes one morning. It was let back into service that afternoon but it soon gave more trouble. It was sent back to depot again and split up into two units. Each was coupled to a unit taken from another train. If the trouble occurred again, this would show which unit was causing the problem. It did and it was eventually found to have an earthing, frayed wire.

A design feature of the 1938 stock was the provision of shed receptacles on both sides of the train. These receptacles are used to provide power inside sheds where there were no current rails. The power is supplied through twin cables hanging from an overhead trolley track. It was usual to plug in the lead on at least one, often two cars, during pre-service preparation to provide current for MGs and compressors. The compressors were particularly important, since it always took time to replenish the air supply during brake and door testing.

Prior to leaving the shed the guard had to remove the leads before the driver started to move the train. Once the leads were removed only the leading car, which was positioned outside the shed over the current rails, had power. It was used to pull out the rest of the train. If the guard forgot to take out the leads they would be dragged along to the end of the shed and jerked out of the receptacles as the train left. The damage caused on such occasions could be quite severe – to the train, to the shed and to the trolley system. Trains were always recalled to the depot after such incidents and drivers, who were deemed to be the responsible party, were dealt with under the due processes of the disciplinary procedure.

In the case of 1938 stock, they had receptacles boxes on both sides of the train and although it was usual to insert leads on one side only, incidents did occur when the other side was used and then forgotten causing embarrassment for the driver and misery for the depot staff who had to sort out the mess.

1938 tube stock in the maintenance shed at Morden depot on 25th June 1958. Those trains set further back from the buffer stops have the cars at the other end standing outside the shed with their shoes on the current rails. Those nearer the stops are 'off juice'. LT Museum

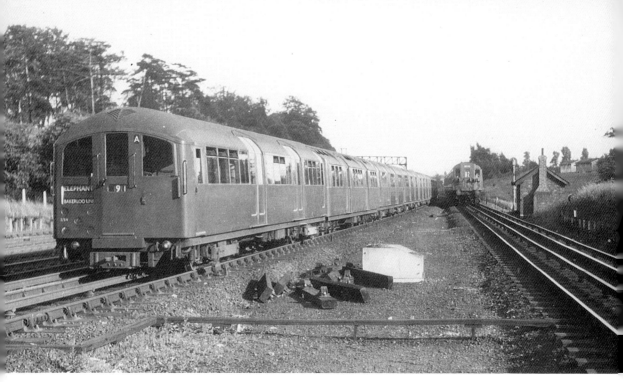

A Bakerloo train passes a BR (LMR) Watford train near Carpenders Park C.R.L. Coles

During the 1960s, a number of 1938 tube cars were fitted with two-tier armrests of the type shown here as a trial prior to their adoption on 1967 tube stock. LT Museum

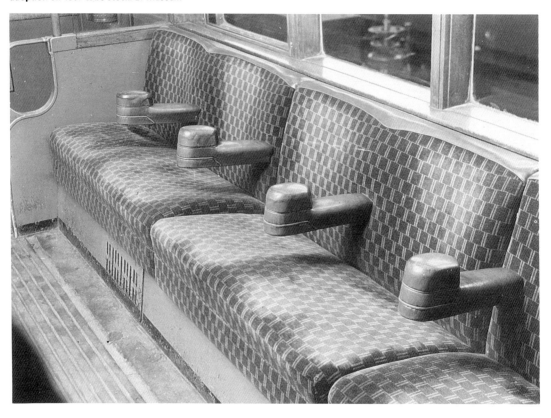

Drayton Park station and depot on the Northern City Line, which received 1938 tube stock in 1966 after the section of line north of Drayton Park (Finsbury Park) had been closed in connection with the building of the Victoria Line.
R.J. Greenaway

The Northern City Line

At the beginning of October 1964 a complete set of new timetables was introduced on the London Underground. They showed across the board cuts in services of between 10% and 15%. Falling traffic and staff recruitment difficulties had brought about the cuts and the number of trains in service was reduced on all lines. The Northern service was reduced from 100 to 96 trains and the Bakerloo from 47 to 45. There was also a sharp cutback in trainmen's duties. Some drivers were reduced to working as guards for a time following these cuts and there was some industrial action for a few days in protest at the job losses.

In 1966, by which time things had settled down, the cuts had made a few extra trains of 1938 stock available and, at the same time, the Northern City Line service had been reduced to a Moorgate to Drayton Park Shuttle. The Northern City platforms at Finsbury Park were closed in preparation for its reconstruction and incorporation into the Victoria Line. The Northern City now only needed six trains for service with a couple of spare trains at Drayton Park Depot for maintenance.

It was now a logical step to dispose of the last of the Standard tube stock then running on the Underground and replace it with the surplus 1938 stock. From the end of October 1966, therefore, the Northern City Line service was gradually taken over by single-unit trains of 1938 stock sent to Drayton Park from Highgate. There was some interworking of the old and 'new' stocks (the 1938 stock was, by then, almost 30 years old) until November 3rd 1966 when the last of the Standard stock left. The normal allocation for 1938 stock was then six units – 3 x 3-cars and 3 x 4-cars, with five of the units being required for service. A spare train was kept at Drayton Park, although no maintenance was done there apart from the daily safety check and cleaning and the weekly examination.

Stock was transferred to Drayton Park from Highgate Wood sidings over the Eastern Region lines. A midday stabling train (which had originated from Golders Green or Morden Depot that day) was left at Highgate Woods and the unit intended for Drayton Park was uncoupled from it and taken to the Northern City by battery locomotive. Care had to be taken that the train used did not include an UNDM. The train at Highgate was restored to its normal length for the evening peak service by the return of the battery locomotive from Drayton Park with another unit.

The train formation on the line was increased to 6-cars when the Victoria Line Stage I opened in September 1968. Trains were still supplied from the Northern Line, whose allocation had been increased

85

by nine units to cover the Northern City work. However, this was changed from the end of September 1970 when the stock was supplied from Neasden. This change came about because of the poor condition of the bridges on the transfer route between Highgate Woods and Drayton Park. It was not considered worth repairing them at the time, and the route has since much changed as a result of the Great Northern electrification scheme. The Bakerloo stock allocation, which had been 52 x 7-cars since 1967, was increased by 6 x 6-cars. The provision of stock for the Northern City had always been a simple operation allowing the use of any available unit from the Northern Line. The route maps inside the cars showing the Northern Line had always included the Northern City since it had always been intended (under the 1935-40 New Works Programme) to have integrated services between the lines. This was never achieved but the map arrangement was convenient while Northern Line 1938 stock was used.

When Bakerloo 1938 stock was introduced, it was a different matter. Bakerloo cars did not have maps showing the Northern City. It therefore became necessary to allocate units specially for the Northern City. They were based at Neasden and sent to Drayton Park between a pair of battery locomotives via the Metropolitan Line, Baker Street, reversing at Barbican (City Widened Lines) and then to King's Cross Suburban.

This transfer was carried out between the peaks but only on certain days of the week. On one occasion the transfer train arrived at Baker Street (Met) on its way to Barbican and stopped in platform 3 awaiting clearance on to the Circle Line. The driver leant out of the cab and called a greeting across to the station master who happened to be standing outside his office on platform 2. The station master who, a former driver himself, had been a colleague of the train driver at Drayton Park years earlier, exchanged some ribald comments with him including one where the driver said 'You were no good as a driver, so they must have a hard time here with you as SM.' Before the SM could reply he heard the telephone ring and dashed into his office to answer it. Soon he reappeared. He coolly stepped over to the edge of the platform and looked back towards the rear of the train. 'George' he called, 'You're not too good yourself. That was the signalman on the phone. You've left some of your train at Finchley Road!' The rear battery loco had become detached from the transfer unit and had stopped in the tunnel just south of Finchley Road. The coupler had parted and the brake pipe had never been properly connected. There were some very red faces that day, not least the driver's!

The normal Drayton Park allocation remained at 6 x 6-car trains. Services continued at the usual 5-train maximum until the line was closed on 4th October 1975. The line was handed over to British Railways for the conversion work to incorporate it into the Great Northern electrification scheme. It was reopened by them on 16th August 1976 when a new shuttle service was started up with dual voltage Great Northern stock.

The 1938 stock and the Northern City Line had the unfortunate distinction of being involved in the worst train accident ever to occur on the London Underground. At 08.46 on Friday 28th February 1975 a 6-car train led by unit 10175-012263-11175 overran the platform of the Northern City terminus at Moorgate at an estimated 35 m.p.h. and hit the wall 120 feet beyond. The driver and 42 passengers died. The rescue operation took four days. The cause of the accident was never satisfactorily explained but mechanical failure was ruled out. A result of the accident was the installation of elaborate (some would say over-elaborate) terminal protection facilities all over the Underground.

A view from the buffer stop at Moorgate (Northern City Line) in June 1972. The neighbouring platform was the scene of a major disaster in 1975 when a driver failed to stop. R.J. Greenaway

Chapter 7
The Question of Replacement

During the five years or so preceding the opening of the Victoria Line in 1968 most of LT's rolling stock design effort had been concentrated on the new trains for that line, the 1967 Tube Stock, and the problems of introducing automatic train operation (ATO). Other things had taken a back seat until it was realised that, with virtually 30 years of service behind it, the bulk of the 1938 stock was due for renewal in five or so years time. At the same time, the Q surface stock cars were also due for replacement. Their replacement had to come first as they had mostly entered service before the 1938 tube cars and this was started with the introduction of the C69 stock from September 1970. In the meantime the question of what to do about the tube stock was considered. There were a number of problems which had to be borne in mind:

*The 1938 stock was not all the same age. The 1949 cars were barely 20 years old. Should these be replaced as well as the 1938 cars?
*Money was tight and it was also considered unlikely that Central Government would give a large batch of new cars to LT just before the Greater London Council was to take over control.
*The Bakerloo and Northern stock could be replaced completely but what about the fifteen 1938 trains on the Piccadilly? The Standard stock on that line had been replaced with 1959 stock and, to get standardisation, should more 1959 stock be ordered to replace these 15 trains even though its design was already out of date?
*An extension of the Piccadilly Line to Heathrow was planned. Did an opportunity exist here for a reshuffle of stock by replacing the Piccadilly's 38s and 59s with new stock and moving the 59s to the Northern? If this option was chosen should some 1938 stock be left on the Northern to work with the 1959 stock or should the numbers be made up by ordering more (obsolete) 1959/62 stock?
*A scheme to build a new tube line – the Fleet Line – from Baker Street to south east London was being floated. What effect would this have on 1938 replacement plans?
*Something had to be done quickly because the KLL4 compressors still in use on many 1938 cars were continuing to give trouble and by this time (1969) up to 15 trains a day were being cancelled because of them.

Various options were considered, including deferring the purchase of new cars until the Heathrow extension was authorised and rehabilitating some cars until the Fleet Line plans had been finalised. The experiments in articulation with the two 1935 motor cars (mentioned earlier) were carried out in 1969 and these were awaiting completion while discussions continued on the tube lines rolling stock programme and the design that future stock would take.

In the meantime, another factor had arisen. A gradual deterioration in the industrial relations position at Acton Works had occurred over the previous year which culminated in a strike beginning in September 1969 which lasted for three months. Sporadic industrial action had taken place during the summer of that year and overhauls of cars and equipment had already fallen behind schedule. As a result there were regular cancellations of trains. Almost as soon as the strike began, further cancellations occurred and by the beginning of October 1969 they had risen to the staggering rate of over 40 a day just for 1938 tube stock on the Northern Line. The majority of these cancellations were due to compressor shortages.

A further deterioration in the situation was prevented by reducing the length of some trains to six cars. Their NDMs were withdrawn and stored. This allowed a compressor to be saved as it was considered necessary to have three compressors on a 7-car train but it was sufficient to allow only two on a 6-car train. Some 6-car trains were run on both the Bakerloo and Northern from this time, until the early 1970s on the Northern and as late as 1978 on the Bakerloo. The Piccadilly lost many of its fifteen 1938 trains by their transfer to the Northern and Bakerloo and was down to only five trains by the end of 1969. It recovered three during the following year but never had more than eight from then on.

Discussion over the replacement or rehabilitation of the 1938 stock continued into 1970. In January of that year the Greater London Council took over control of London Transport. Almost anyone who had any influence within LT (and many others who didn't) produced his own plan for the future of Underground rolling stock based on informed assumptions and best guesses as to what GLC and Government policy would turn out to be. There was considerable confusion. In the midst of all this the London Evening Standard dubbed the Northern Line 'The Misery Line'.

Occasionally, cars transferred from the Northern to other lines arrived the wrong way round. This train of 1938 stock arrived at Northfields with the 'D' end facing west instead of east. It was turned, with the author as driver, on Sunday 26th July 1970, using the triangle of lines between Earl's Court (District), High Street Kensington (reverse) and South Kensington (reverse). It is seen here leaving Earl's Court having completed its triangular trip. R.J. Greenaway

During the mid-1970s, various new systems for lifting and moving cars within depots were examined. Here, a 1938 trailer car is seen being moved on an air cushion system during experiments in the old lifting shop at White City depot. The idea was not considered worth adopting. R.J. Greenaway Collection

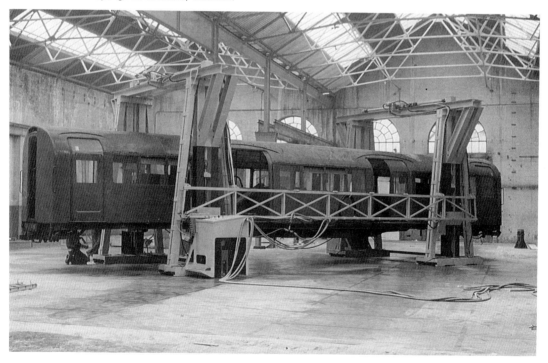

In truth the press, and the public, had good cause for complaint. An LT report summed things up by saying 'A ride on the Northern Line today is a depressing experience, with dirty rolling stock, filthy stations and little or no platform attendance, all of which gives the impression that nobody cares. When this is coupled with overcrowding, public complaints are inevitable'.

The industrial troubles and the acute staff shortage which had developed by this time were having a serious effect on both operating and maintenance performance. The political changes only added to the problems. It was not until early in April 1970 that the newly appointed LT executive got round to making a decision about rolling stock. They decided to ask the GLC for authority to buy new stock for the Piccadilly Line in anticipation of the authorisation of the Heathrow extension. The plan also included moving the 1959 stock to the Northern and rehabilitating 88 trains of 1938 stock for continued service. The rehabilitation would include rewiring and painting the cars in 1959 colours to allow both stocks to work in multiple. The idea of providing more 1959/62 stock to make up the balance of trains required for the Northern Line was abandoned at this time.

In choosing this plan a number of other ideas were firmed up. Articulation was still considered a possibility but its development was not advanced enough to allow mass production for the Piccadilly Line in time for the Heathrow opening. The Piccadilly was to get 6-car trains using a new design of long car but giving an overall shorter train length. The idea was that the whole train should be fully within the platform to allow door control from the cabs; from the rear of a two-man train or from the front of a one-man train. The articulated trains would be for the Fleet Line and would eventually replace the rehabilitated 1938 stock on the Bakerloo. It was expected that the new Piccadilly stock would be delivered after the C69 surface stock, then under construction, and that the programme would be complete by 1976.

By the time that these proposals were formally put to the GLC in May 1970, a new alternative had been included. Instead of rehabilitating 88 trains of 1938 stock, only 58 were to be done. The shortfall of 30 was to be made up by purchasing 30 x 7 car trains of new stock based on the Victoria Line's 1967 stock. The new trains were not to be fitted with ATO since they were to be run on the Northern with the 1959 stock after its transfer from the Piccadilly. It was LT's policy at this time to purchase all new rolling stock with future conversion to ATO in mind and the decision not to do so for this new stock, which became the 1972 (MkI) tube stock, was said by some to be a retrograde step.

The decision to go for new trains instead of using rehabilitated 1938 stock to run with 1959 stock on the Northern was political. There was considerable pressure on LT at the time from their masters at the GLC to demonstrate that 'they were doing something' about conditions on the Northern. In their original rehabilitation scheme for the 1938 stock, the Acton design staff had intended that 1938 units would be rewired to allow them to couple with 1959 stock, they would get fluorescent lighting and would be painted silver to match. It was considered necessary that they should last long enough to enable them to be replaced in a batch with the 1959 stock. The year 1994 was quoted as a possibility at the time. In accepting the pressure to introduce a batch of new trains, LT had obviously abandoned the idea of continuing operation of the Northern with interchangeable stock. With the introduction of the 1972 stock there would always be at least two types of stock running on the line.

The GLC, who had only taken control of LT from January 1970, were understandably cautious. They had no experience of running a large transport undertaking and they were suspicious of the workings of such a complex and apparently independent body as London Transport. Two months after LT's revised plans were submitted in May 1970 for new Piccadilly and Northern stock and the rehabilitation of 58 trains of 1938 stock, they decided to authorise only the purchase of the 1972 stock. They decided to wait for Government approval of the extension to Heathrow before proceeding with the rest of the programme.

A view of 10011-11011 at Acton Works in August 1970 during the period of articulation tests. The two bodies were cut back at their trailing ends and mounted on a single bogie. R.J. Greenaway

In the meantime the GLC asked for a reappraisal of the rehabilitation programme. Since the idea to make the 1938 stock compatible with the 1959 stock had fallen by the wayside, there was not much point in spending money on that part of the programme. Those running on the Bakerloo did not need these modifications anyway. A revised cost estimate, which cut the original cost almost in half, appeared in November 1970. In the same month the Government approved the Heathrow extension.

Almost a year elapsed before anything further happened. Then it all happened within the space of a few weeks. First, the purchase of the 1973 tube stock for the Piccadilly Line was at long last approved in July 1971. Then, the construction of the Fleet Line was authorised. The Great Northern electrification scheme, which included the takeover of the Northern City Line by BR, was also given the go-ahead. Finally, the GLC approved the LT plans to rehabilitate the 1938 tube stock.

**A 7-car Bakerloo
train enters Canons
Park southbound
c.1970**. R.J.
Greenaway Collection

The year's delay had had several consequences. The construction of the 30 x 7 cars of 1972 stock for the Northern Line was already well under way and would be completed long before the designs for 1973 stock were ready for their construction to commence. The gap in production which this created would cause serious financial problems for the builders, Metro-Cammell, who were facing a recession and had no other work in the pipeline. LT was already aware of the parlous state of Metro-Cammell, who were the only British car builders then left in business, and had carried out a survey of European car builders during 1970 to see how many of them were capable of completing the Piccadilly Line order if Metro-Cammell closed down.

The plan for the Fleet Line (now the Jubilee Line) was that it would connect at Baker Street with the Bakerloo branch to Stanmore and allow the Bakerloo to revert to its former single route from Elephant to Queens Park and Watford. The Bakerloo Line would then require 33 trains. This was also the number of trains required to work the authorised Fleet Line

(Stage I) service between Charing Cross and Stanmore. If more stock was ordered now, so the thinking at that time went, it would allow continuous production at Metro-Cammell's, it would provide new stock for Stage I of the Fleet Line and, when further stages of the Fleet Line were completed and more stock was needed, a new Fleet Line stock would be built, and the trains working on Stage I would be transferred to the Bakerloo and replace the remaining 1938 stock. While the Fleet Line was being built, the new stock could be used on the Northern and allow more rapid removal of the 1938 stock. With the politically unacceptable demise of Metro-Cammell facing them and with so many benefits accruing from a second order for new stock, the Government had little choice. The 33 extra trains were authorised and they became known as the 1972 MkII stock.

Three generations of stock at Edgware depot; 1959, 1938 and 1972 MkII.

To recap, we must look back to the original proposals of April 1970. It was suggested then that, of the 180 trains of 1938 stock then available, 90 would be replaced by new Piccadilly stock and 88 would be rehabilitated. The difference of two trains would be made up reducing the total of spare trains required on the Northern by rewiring rehabilitated 38s to allow them to couple with 1959 stock. The numbers were then whittled down as follows:

Total of 1938 tube stock trains then extant:	180
less 90 to be replaced by 1973 tube stock:	(-90)
less 2 saved by reduced spares on Northern:	(-2)
Total stock originally intended for rehabilitation:	88
less 30 to be replaced by 1972 MkI tube stock:	(-30)
less 6 saved by transfer of Northern City line:	(-6)
less 18 saved by transfer of Stanmore Branch from Bakerloo:	(-18)
Final total of 1938 stock for rehabilitation	34

The final figure of 34 trains was the number of 1938 stock trains which were now to be rehabilitated under the revised programme.

It will be recalled that the original total of 1938 stock trains available after the 1949 uncoupling programme was completed in 1953 was 184 x 7-cars (1288 cars). By April 1970 this had been reduced to 172 x 7-cars and 8 x 6-cars in line with the reduced services and the revised information for the Northern City Line. Although the total of cars in regular service had been reduced by 36, only eight cars had been recorded as scrapped. The remainder were still extant on the system in one form or another, many stored awaiting a decision on the rehabilitation programme.

EHO

The plans for the rehabilitation of the 1938 tube stock had already been drawn up well in advance of formal authority to proceed and, in fact, a 4-car unit (10284-012374-12144-11284) was given a trial rehabilitation early in 1971. It was completed in late March, sent to Golders Green and inspected there by various interested parties. A significant additional improvement was suggested as a result of these inspections. It was decided to add door fault indicator lights. This was not originally done on this unit but was added later. It became standard on rehabilitated units and was virtually the only way in which they could be distinguished from other units by the outside observer.

The rehabilitation programme, which became known as EHO (Extra Heavy Overhaul) was finally agreed in early 1971 and it envisaged the completion of the work in mid-1974. The next unit entered the works in September 1971 and was completed in December. Various technical problems and the chronic staff shortages had conspired to delay the work. Production continued during 1972 and 1973 but by the end of 1973 only 20 of the 34 trains had been done. There had been more staff trouble at Acton and by May 1974 there was another dispute which caused a stoppage of EHO work altogether. This lasted until early in 1975. The programme was not completed until December 1976.

Although it had not been intended to put EHO trains on to the Northern, many were used there until late 1974 and the Bakerloo had very few EHO trains until then. The last EHO train from the Northern Line was transferred to the Bakerloo on 12th November 1974.

The progress of the EHO work was accompanied by various changes in livery. The first sign of this was the appearance of a 4-car unit (10218-012304-12422-11218) on the Northern Line in October 1972 sporting a lighter shade of red than normal. This unit had undergone a normal heavy overhaul at Acton and had been finished in 'bus red' in anticipation of the standardisation of LT's bus and rail paints. It retained its standard gold numbers and fleet names.

It is worth noting at this point that when EHO's started, normal overhauls were stopped for a time. The last Northern Line unit (10170) left Acton on 14th October 1971 and the last Bakerloo (10106) and 22nd October. However, since some non-EHO units were expected to remain in service for up to five more years, another twenty were given overhauls between September 1972 and June 1973. In addition, five units then based on the East London Line were given overhauls during 1975.

The units outshopped from Acton after the appearance of 10218 unit in bus red livery continued to have the standard train red and gold lettering until February 1973. From that time, all EHO units leaving Acton, starting with unit 10208, had a large white LT roundel and white car numbers applied but they retained the standard train red body colour. Surprisingly, the 'NO ENTRANCE' transfers over cab doors continued to be of the old gold pattern, as did the car numbers displayed inside the driving cabs and those used to replace missing number plates inside the passenger saloons.

In November 1973, another livery change took place. EHO units, beginning with unit 10184, were turned out in bus red livery with white roundels and lettering. This continued until the last was done in December 1976. By this time, two odd units had appeared, 10012 and 10321. These both had 1949 stock trailers (012495 and 012503 respectively) which had been included in the EHO programme in error, since it was intended to eliminate all non-standard vehicles. To correct the error, two 1938 trailers (012256 and 012380) were EHO'd in June 1976. They were finished in bus red but replaced cars which were in two train red units. The resulting mixed livery survived in these two units until 1977 when both were given a normal overhaul, excepting the two trailers.

As already mentioned, non-EHO units continued to get overhauls between September 1972 and June 1973. These units retained the train red and gold transfers. However, the East London Line units were given ordinary overhauls between February and November 1975 and they had bus red and white roundels and numbers. They were also fitted with stabling lights. The provision of these was begun for EHO units only in June 1973. Its application was very gradual and it was 1979 before they were all done.

In June 1976 EHO units began to receive normal overhauls, some having been in service for five years since rehabilitation. The first unit to be done was the prototype 10284. By early in 1979, the last of the 26 EHO units which had run in the train red/gold transfer livery (10214) underwent overhaul. It last ran on the Bakerloo on 12th February 1979 before going to Acton the next day. Overhauls of 1938 stock finally ceased in 1982.

One modification which appeared on the EHO trains but which was not part of the EHO programme was the provision of train radio. Trials were carried out on the Bakerloo and Hammersmith and Circle Lines during 1972-3 with a new form of driver-to-control communication system known as Storno Radio. The 'Storno' name was that of the company which supplied the equipment. The existing DRICO (Driver-to-Controller) system had been introduced during the early 1950s and suffered from the disadvantage that the train had to be stopped to allow a physical connection between the train and tunnel wires for communication to be established. The Storno system made use of a 'leaky feeder' aerial system in the tunnels which allowed communication whilst on the move. The trials were a success and, in 1977, work began on fitting the equipment to the outer end cabs of each 7-car train of EHO stock. They were provided with the necessary equipment, which included a microphone with a foot operated switch, to allow the driver to keep both hands on the driving and braking controls, and an external aerial near the top of the offside cab window. The work was completed early in 1979.

The original purpose of EHO was to allow the stock to run for a further ten years without a further deterioration in reliability and to improve upon that reliability if at all possible. Much discussion took place during the two years leading up to the start of work in 1971 as how best to achieve these objectives and what might be done to improve the image and operation of the stock. Much discussion has also taken place since as to whether the scheme was successful and what might have been done or not do instead, especially since the original programme was to have cost £1.4 million but actually ended up costing over £2 million for the original 34 trains.

Initially, of course, there was much uncertainty as to what the role of the stock was to be. If it was to remain in use in large numbers, as the original plan for the 88 trains envisaged, its visibility would have been widespread and a more visual modernisation would have been called for. This would have included repainting in 'silver' paint and the provision of new upholstery and fluorescent lighting. The provision of fluorescent lighting would have involved replacing the existing motor generator, which could only provide a DC output. Fluorescent lighting preferred an AC output. The cost of this was high and was not considered worth it for the reduced number of trains eventually decided upon for rehabilitation. The existing tungsten lighting remained. It was considered good when the stock was new, even with the fluted glass shades which were removed in 1960-61 because of the problems of replacing them when broken. However, in more recent times, the introduction of fluorescent lighting left tungsten-lit cars looking rather dingy compared with modern stock, until an attempt was made to brighten them up in 1980 by increasing the bulbs from 45 to 60 watts.

The initial uncertainty concerning the use of the stock was particularly obvious when the car wiring was considered. At first, complete rewiring was proposed. The existing wiring was rubber covered and it had become brittle with age causing electrical failures. Only some places were badly affected but it was suggested that, if complete rewiring were done, the trains could be modified to enable them to couple with 1959/62 stock. This would have been done in conjunction with repainting and relighting but, once it was decided that the EHO cars would not be required to run on the Northern for any length of time, nor couple with 1959 stock, the whole idea was dropped and the rewiring was confined to the most vulnerable areas.

One of these vulnerable areas was the wiring bundle under 'J' door which separated the driver's cab from the passenger saloon. Insulation breakdown at this point was often the cause of electrical problems and sometimes a drastic remedy was used in order to effect a temporary repair and prevent a train being cancelled. In this case, a quantity of grey insulating paint, of the type used on shoebeams was poured over the offending wiring to replace the damaged insulation until time and labour could be found to do a more permanent job.

Easier everyday maintenance and reduction of failures were the prime targets of the EHO programme as finally carried out. There were various technical tasks, largely unseen by the passenger, such as the rewiring mentioned above and the renewal of pipework where

The rear of a seven-car train at Queen's Park, showing the Storno radio aerial and also the rarely seen 'Piccadilly' destination plate, in use because of engineering work taking place between Waterloo and Embankment. Brian Hardy

necessary, the fitting of new traction motor bearings and installing reciprocating compressors where not already provided. There were also bodywork jobs like the renewal of floor lagging, door runners, door rubber edges, new window glass and new hinged door locks. Much of the original window glass still showed the chipping caused by the removal of the wartime safety netting. This all disappeared after the completion of EHO. During EHO also, the passenger tip-up seats on the NDMs and trailers were removed to improve access on crowded trains and, as already mentioned, door fault indicator lights were fitted.

Some improvements to the driving cabs were added as work progressed. An additional heater was installed, improved draught proofing was provided and a sun visor was added. The brake and traction controllers were painted in 'C69 grey', apparently in an attempt to distinguish them from non-EHO cabs. The guard was provided with twin pilot lights (one on each door control panel) in place of the single, ceiling-mounted lamp which had been standard on the 1938 stock. The twin lamp idea was simply a way of preventing a train's withdrawal from service if one lamp failed. It was first standardised on the R stock and had also appeared on 12 cars of 1938 stock on the Northern Line in 1969 as an experiment. The 12 cars were the DMs at the outer ends of six trains. The lamps were fitted on the ventilator grille housing over the end communicating door. Towards the end of 1970, it was decided to modify all trains in the same way but to place the bulbs in the guard's panels. For the first few modified cars, the panel mounted bulbs were placed in the holes formerly occupied by the orange 'passenger open' lights. These had, in many cases, been covered with metal plates and, when attempts were made to re-use the holes, it proved more difficult than had been envisaged. Eventually, the conversion involved the drilling of new holes. Not all trains had been done when EHO started and it was then confined to EHO trains only.

The proof of the pudding is, as the saying goes, in the eating. Looked at from this point of view, the success or otherwise of the EHO programme could only be determined by performance compared with non-EHO trains operating under the same conditions. In 1975, when a comparison between the failure rates of EHO and non-EHO cars were made, the improvement was measured at 12½% in favour of EHO cars. By 1978 the failure rate had risen to an extent where it was virtually the same as on non-EHO cars. As a result, it was decided to give two more trains the EHO treatment in an attempt to overcome the shortage of serviceable trains. On these two trains the tip-up seats on the trailers and NDMs were retained. The failure rate continued to rise and, by 1981, it was double the rate recorded for non-EHO stock in the days when EHO was first proposed.

Whilst it is easy to be wise with hindsight, there would seem to be some evidence to show that the EHO programme was not as successful as it should have been. To begin with, the attempt to modernise the stock by repainting, reupholstering and installing fluorescent lighting, was quashed on the grounds of expense. This may have been a mistake, because it would have allowed more reliable electrical equipment to be installed and it would have provided a much better visual indication of the improvements. It would have shown both passengers and staff that money had been spent. As it was, the EHO trains were only discernible to the most observant by the evidence of door fault indicator lights. In other respects they looked just like any other train fresh from overhaul. Even the new livery, when it appeared, did not help. Whilst the desire to standardise paint supplies can be understood, the bus red did not sit well on Underground rolling stock, having an orange hue. This was made worse by the application of the white logo and numbers which replaced the quality of gold lettering with garish modernity. The unfortunate story of the design fiasco which London Transport suffered during the early 1970s was the result of the work done by the Design Research Unit under the direction of the late Professor Sir Misha Black. His work with the design of the rolling stock and stations on the Victoria Line was widely acclaimed but he was prevented from putting a large red bar-and-circle logo under the cab windows of the 1967 tube stock by direct intervention from the London Transport Executive. He took his 'revenge' following the formation of the LT Board in 1971, when his team was allowed to desecrate the world famous LT symbol by splashing blobs of white paint on the side of red trains, followed by the ultimate stupidity, painting the doors of the otherwise unpainted 1972 MkII stock red.

On the technical side, it might have improved matters if more work had been carried out on modernising the e.p. brake system and on overhauling the PCM equipment. The latter had always had a good reliability record but it began to age rather quickly from the mid-1970s and the low priority it had been given during EHO became a liability. There also seems to have been trouble with quality control at Acton. Some jobs were not done properly and some were missed altogether. Also at this time, there were staff shortages and too many industrial troubles and there is no doubt that the management was under considerable difficulties. It is not surprising that quality began to slip.

It is interesting to note that during the discussions which preceded the decision to do the rehabilitation, reference was made to previous attempts to improve reliability in this way. The Standard stock rehabilitation of stored cars during 1946-7 and that of the F stock in 1951-2 were quoted as examples of previous schemes which had cost more money than budgeted and which had not given the reliability hoped for. However, both stocks lasted until 1963 – another ten years life had been obtained. For the 1938 stock too, another ten years of life – longer in fact – was achieved. If the reliability was not what was hoped for, how much worse would it have been without EHO?

Chapter 8
The Beginning of the End

Following the authorisation in the summer of 1971 of the EHO programme for the 34 trains of 1938 stock and the replacement of the remainder by new 1972 and 1973 stocks, a rolling stock replacement programme was drawn up. It was expected that Stage I of the Fleet Line, as the Jubilee Line was still then called, would be opened in 1977. In the meantime, 63 trains of 1972 Stock would enter service on the Northern, displacing an equal number of 1938 stock trains, followed by 88 trains of 1973 stock for the Piccadilly. The 1956/9/62 stock on the Piccadilly would be displaced to the Northern as the 1973 stock arrived. The first 1959 stock arrivals on the Northern would allow the remaining 30-odd trains of 1938 stock to be withdrawn from that line, followed by the transfer of 1972 MkII stock, first to the Bakerloo, then to the Fleet Line. During the delivery of the 1972 stock, the 34 trains of 1938 stock would receive their EHO. Although it overran by two years, this was largely how the programme was carried out.

Part of the programme involved the scrapping of 1938 stock. It was based on the premise that all non-standard cars would be eliminated first and remaining cars would be selected for withdrawal on the basis of their mileage and general condition. The best cars would be reserved for EHO. An equal number of 3-car and 4-car units had to be EHO'd at any one time because of the need to keep them together in the same train. The modifications to the door circuits prevented EHO units from being coupled to non-EHO units in passenger service.

The first part of the scrapping plan covered the removal of 210 cars – the 30 x 7-car trains to be replaced by 1972 MkI stock. It incorporated a scheme of reformations to leave the remaining trains in the original 1938 formations of M-NDM-T-M and M-T-M. The cars to be scrapped were:

91	UNDM cars
29	DM cars
52	1927 (58) trailers
8	1935 trailers
30	NDM cars
210	= 30 x 7 cars

This programme allowed the scrapping of all the UNDMs and 58 trailers, of which 52 of the latter were left by this time. The other six were withdrawn between 1963 and 1970. Three driving motors and two trailers had also been scrapped. One each of the motors and trailers had been casualties of the accident at Tooting Broadway on 6th October 1960, when a driver mistakenly accelerated south from the station thinking he was going to Morden but was actually routed into the siding. Parts from these cars (11103 and 012488) were used until 1988 to provide a mock-up of air door equipment at the White City Railway Training Centre. A similar loss of a motor and a trailer occurred in an almost identical accident at the same place on 4th May 1971. In this instance, the driver died of his injuries.

The total of 91 UNDMs due for scrapping was one fewer than the number built because one (30001) had been converted into a trailer and renumbered 012516 in 1964 as a result of a series of unit reformations after collisions. Other conversions during this period included two in 1966, when NDM 12151 became trailer 012151 and 012517 was created from the undamaged trailing ends of collision cars 11073 and 10296, and one in 1970 when 12022 became 012022.

All these changes had reduced the number of 1938 stock cars on the books by twelve and this figure was increased to 15 early in 1972 by the scrapping of three motor cars. A further 21 cars were scattered about the system out of service leaving the following cars operational:

Bakerloo:	50 x 7-cars
	1 x 6-cars
Northern City:	6 x 6-cars
Northern:	114 x 7-cars
	1 x 3-cars
Piccadilly:	8 x 7-cars
Total:	1249 cars

The first train of 1972 MkI stock entered service on the Northern Line on 26th June 1972 and the bulk removal of 1938 stock began in the same month. A pattern of stock transfers began to appear whereby a

A '58 trailer' in a southbound Bakerloo train at Wembley Park. The car beyond is an UNDM. K. Harris

train of 1938 stock was sent from the Northern to Neasden where it was reformed, if required, to keep any good cars. The trains sent invariably had a 3-car unit with an UNDM. Upon arrival at Neasden, the unit with the UNDM was paired with its corresponding Bakerloo unit (e.g. 10043-70568-31001 and 30017-012404-11043), the cars for scrapping removed and a new unit with a matching motor car pair formed: 10043-012404-11043. The 4-car unit sent over with the UNDM unit was often reduced to 3-cars by removal of the NDM so that it could replace a 3-car Bakerloo unit containing a '58' trailer. Scrap cars were taken into the lifting shop at Neasden, where any useful equipment was removed and were then formed up into (normally) 7-car sets for removal to the scrap dealers. Initially, they were taken direct by BR from Neasden to the Long Marston works of Birds, the scrap dealers. Fol-

lowing the opening of the spur between the Metropolitan Line and Ruislip Depot in July 1973, scrap trains were sent there for collection by BR. In addition to Birds, Kings of Newmarket and Booths of Rotherham also dealt with a large number of cars and smaller jobs went to Cashmores and Cohens. A few cars, usually accident victims, were cut up on site or at a depot.

In September 1973, the last of the '58' trailers (70534) was withdrawn and sent for scrap and two months later the last UNDM (31030) followed the same path. On 19th November 1973, the first of the 1972 MkII trains entered service and although withdrawals of 1938 stock continued on the Northern Line and trains continued to be transferred to Neasden for disposal, some units were held back from immediate scrapping. This was largely because of the decision to introduce 1938 stock on the East London Line.

1938 trailer 012193 at Acton Works following its return from Metro-Cammell in 1976. The car was used for ventilation trials from 1974. It was scrapped in 1980. Brian Hardy

1938 stock was introduced on the East London Line in January 1973. Prior to this, a train for crew training was kept at Whitechapel, stabled in the westbound siding as seen here. LURS

Motor car 10319 of a 1938 stock EHO unit at Wembley Park painted in bus red livery with white roundels and numbers. Note the door fault indicator light on the roof near the first pair of doors. This was the only way to distinguish EHO units of 1938 stock. Brian Hardy

London Transport had traditionally used a darker shade of red for its Underground stock compared to road vehicles. By 1973, with most Underground trains being unpainted, the remaining 1938 stock started to receive 'bus' red during EHO at Acton. The two shades are seen side by side at Finchley Road. Capital Transport

Interior of trailer 012211 towards the end of its working life, showing the final interior colour scheme of most of the 1938 stock. Capital Transport

Because of a shortage of serviceable CO/CP 'surface' stock for the East London Line service, dedicated four-car units of 1938 Tube Stock were employed on this service between 1974 and 1977. One such is seen at Rotherhithe. Fred Ivey

The East London Line

The early 1970s was a trying time for the London Underground. There was a continuing staff shortage caused by the unpopularity of shift work, the lower than average wages and the general disdain held by the public for work in public services. There were several upheavals in the organisation due to the take-over by the GLC and by the decision to combine LT's bus and rail engineering organisations. Uncertainty over the Fleet Line funding and its effect on the rolling stock renewal programme plus the instability caused by the opposing political colours of the GLC and Government also had a debilitating effect on the organisation. The trades unions were often able to take advantage of the situation and, at Acton Works in particular, there were constant petty disputes. Some were the result of inter-union rivalry, some were directly aimed at the management. One of these disputes was partially responsible for the introduction of 1938 stock on the East London Line.

The East London was a surface stock line and had used Metropolitan or District stock at various times since its electrification in 1913. It usually got the 'leftovers' of one or other of the surface lines' stock depending on the situation at the time and, since 1971, it had used District Line CO and CP stock. However, this stock had recently suffered a number of cases of fractured wheel spokes, the most serious of which resulted in a derailment at Victoria one evening which had repercussions on the service for the next four days.

The situation created a wheel shortage on the District which was aggravated by the aforementioned dispute at Acton. Train cancellations on the District were running into double figures daily and the prospect of another 'Misery Line' press campaign was a real possibility. The delivery of the 1972 stock was progressing well on the Northern and there were obvious and considerable improvements on that line. It would be a disaster to lose the recovered goodwill by allowing another 'Misery Line' to appear. The 1972 MkII stock provided the answer. Its delivery was continuing to release 1938 stock which, it was decided, could be used on the East London Line. It would replace the CO/CP stock for use on the District and would help to ease the effects of the wheel shortage.

It was decided to proceed with this scheme in October 1973. Crew training began shortly afterwards using an 8-car 1938 stock train (units 10124 & 10126) stabled in the District siding at Whitechapel. The changeover was carried out on 12th/13th January 1974 and from the 13th, 4-car units of 1938 stock began providing the service. It was usual to keep eight units for use on the line – five for service, one spare at New Cross Depot and two at Neasden for mainten-ance. Although they were based at Neasden they were kept separate from the Bakerloo fleet because they were fitted with special East London Line maps and warning notices on the doors which read 'Caution – Step down into train' on the outside and 'Caution –

Step up to platform' inside. This was because of the height difference between the tube car floors and the platforms intended for surface stock trains. Some work on raising the track was done but the step height was still considerable.

One of the units was withdrawn in September 1974 because it was the subject of numerous failures. This was 10082, which was replaced by 10110. In the November, more problems arose when all three off-peak trains were withdrawn from service due to wet and draughty cabs so that by lunch-time there was no service at all. A hurried stock transfer from Neasden was arranged during the afternoon and two Bakerloo units (10118 and 10240) were used with suitably repaired East London units to provide the evening peak service of five trains. From time to time other Bakerloo units appeared on the line. As already mentioned, five of the East London units were given ordinary overhauls at Acton during 1975, doubtless as a result of their poor reliability. Two EHO units were allocated to the East London Line for a time, 10186 between December 1974 and November 1975 and 10162 between July 1976 and June 1977. During these periods they ran with the East London Line maps and notices. The latter unit replaced 10142 which was sent

to Acton for EHO and which never returned to the East London. This was one of four additional units given an EHO so as to increase the allocation of the Bakerloo's 1938 stock from 34 to 36 trains. As mentioned earlier, the extra trains were deemed necessary to order to maintain a reasonable standard of service against the rising failure rate of the stock.

1938 stock continued to work on the East London Line until the weekend of 11th/12th June 1977 when it was replaced by Metropolitan Line A stock. Of the units so displaced, one became part of a test train, two went back to the Bakerloo Line and the other five were scrapped. Of the two which went back to the Bakerloo, one was the EHO unit 10162 and the other was given an EHO and became one of the four extra units so treated.

A 4-car 1938 stock unit arrives at New Cross Gate with a BR train of 4SUB stock stabled in the background. The 1938 stock was built before the 4SUB stock and lasted longer. Capital Transport

Cars allocated to the East London Line were maintained at Neasden and had to have special line diagrams provided. Capital Transport

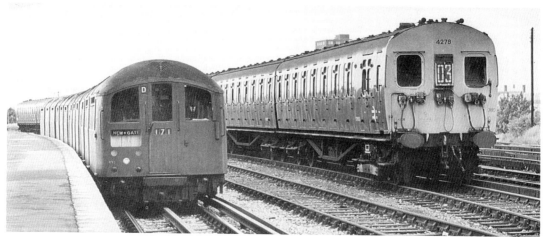

The Piccadilly Line extension to Hatton Cross was opened on 19th July 1975 and the three 1938 stock trains still left on the line had to be provided with Hatton Cross destinations. Here one is seen at Osterley on its way to the new station. Capital Transport

Withdrawals and Conversions

Although the introduction of 1938 stock on the East London Line back in 1974 had temporarily reduced the numbers of cars intended for withdrawal, scrapping had continued virtually unabated. This was largely due to the fact that there was some surplus stock available because of reductions in services. On the Piccadilly Line, for example, the number of trains allocated to the line had dropped by 10% since the late-1960s. From the eight 1938 trains on the line in 1970 the total had dropped to two by July 1974. The last of these ran on 26th July, but in March 1975 one train reappeared. Another was reinstated in April and a third in May. The extension to Hatton Cross was opened on 19th July 1975 and, from this day, the 1938 stock on the Piccadilly had to be provided with destination plates with Hatton Cross labels stuck on them. The three trains remained in use, usually only during the peaks, until 2nd December when the last of them (10029 + 11022) was withdrawn.

The year 1975 saw a hiatus in the 1938 stock scrapping programme. All but one of the 1972 MkII stock trains had entered service on the Northern Line at the end of December 1974. The one odd train was being used by the Design Division for testing purposes and did not enter service until May 1978, when it went directly to the Bakerloo. At the end of December 1974, over 420 cars of 1938 stock had been withdrawn, almost matching the 434 cars of 1972 stock which had entered service. Further withdrawals depended on 1959 stock transferring to the Northern following the arrival of 1973 stock on the Piccadilly. Although the first of this stock entered service in July 1975 for the opening of the Hatton Cross extension, further trains were delayed by considerable technical problems. The first 1959 stock was not released for crew training on the Northern until November 1975 and the first ran in passenger service on 1st December 1975. Withdrawal of 1938 stock then began again in earnest and, over the next year, the numbers of 1938 trains on the Northern dropped from 50 to 26.

By early in November 1977, the last of the non-EHO stock was withdrawn from the Bakerloo. It had been displaced by 1972 MkII stock transferred from the Northern. The first train of the new stock had entered service on the Bakerloo on 4th April 1977 and, by November, there were 17 of them in use on the line.

The 1938 stock on the Bakerloo now consisted of only the 34 EHO trains. By the end of the year, there were only 10½ trains of non-EHO stock left on the Northern and these were all withdrawn over the next four months. As a result, the last (so everyone thought at the time) 1938 stock to run in service on the Northern was on Friday 14th April 1978. The train ran as set 121, 07.17 Morden Depot to 18.16 Golders Green Depot and comprised:

10182-012275-12127-11182+10203-012203-11203

For at time, matters were stabilised for the 1938 stock. Bulk scrapping ceased in the May and, as already noted, two more trains were EHO'd and allocated to the Bakerloo, bringing that line's 1938 stock allocation up to 36 trains.

It had always been the practice on the Underground to use redundant passenger vehicles for non-passenger duties and the 1938 stock was no exception. In June 1973, just one year after the bulk withdrawal of the stock began, driving motors Nos. 10088 and 11067 were converted into Ballast motor cars. Car 10088 originally bore the number L84 but it never ran in service with it and appeared instead as L140. No. 11067 became L141. A total of 17 cars were converted, including another L140, over the next seven years:

Previous No.	New No.	Converted
10088	L140	6/73 (Scrapped 1/79)
10182	L140	9/80 (Withdrawn 1986)
11067	L141	6/73
10021	L142	12/73
10065	L143	12/73
10257	L144	12/75
11027	L145	12/75
10034	L146	11/76
11034	L147	11/76
10022	L148	10/77 (now sold to BR)
11104	L149	10/77 (now sold to BR)
10327	L150	7/78
11327	L151	7/78
10266	L152	5/78
11266	L153	5/78
10141	L154	7/78 (Withdrawn 1986)
11141	L155	9/78 (Scrapped 12/85)

The first L140 was destroyed by fire at Lillie Bridge on the morning of 16th January 1979. It was taken to Acton Works between locos L144 and L145 on 2nd March for scrapping. Upon reaching Acton, in indirectly took its revenge when L144 was uncoupled from it. L144 rolled away and struck A stock trailer 6207 which was coupled to its partners 6206 and 5206. The resulting impact caused 5206 to shove its coupler

When the scrapping of the 1938 stock began in 1972, the opportunity was taken to convert some driving motor cars into Ballast Motors, replacing Pre-1938 Ballast Motors converted in 1954-55 but being of 1923 vintage. Reversing in London Road depot, Bakerloo Line, L149 (formerly 11104) is nearest the camera with the Bakerloo Line stores train. This operated when required to supply equipment to Queen's Park depot, which had no road access. This working ceased when Stonebridge Park depot opened in 1979 and Queen's Park became just a stabling point. *Brian Hardy*

A total of 16 Ballast Motors were converted from 1938 Tube Stock driving motor cars, which included a pair specifically for weed killing duties. L150 and L151 are seen in Ruislip depot in original livery, the pair being originally 90327 and 91327 of the erstwhile nine-car trains scheme of the Northern Line. Brian Hardy

From 1979, the livery adopted for most Underground service locomotives was to become yellow, ballast motor L144 seen in Ealing Common depot being so repainted in June 1980. Brian Hardy

into the front cab door of sleet loco ESL107. This example of rough shunting caused extensive damage to L144 but it was eventually repaired and reappeared in July 1980 in the new yellow livery then being applied to service stock. L150 and L151 were included in the ballast motor numbering series but the were actually converted as weed-killing vehicles.

The 1938 stock ballast locos were not considered as useful as their Standard stock predecessors, principally because they lacked power. The Standard stock cars had two 240 h.p. motors whereas 1938 stock cars had two 168 h.p. motors. There was also more work involved in the conversion of 1938 cars because they had to be equipped with compressors. Standard stock driving motor cars had them already, whereas 1938 stock units always had them on the trailers and NDMs. The 1938 ballast cars had compressors mounted inside the former passenger saloon between one of the double doorways. The double doors were all sealed. The motor generator supplied main lighting and battery fed emergency lighting continued to be provided but the e.p. brake was replaced by the Westinghouse air brake. The automatic couplers at the cab ends and the bar couplers at the trailing ends were replaced by the old type Ward coupler and waist level hose couplings were provided. At the trailing ends only, a pair of jumpers were provided to allow through control of both motor cars on a train. At the driving ends, the original five marker lights were replaced by a pair of lights and a bracket was fitted near the cab roof to allow a special flashing light to be fitted. The cars retained their PCM traction equipment but an extra resistance was inserted in the starting circuit to compensate for the possibility of having to start heavier loads than originally designed for. Inside the cars, the original seating was removed but some wooden seats were provided for staff transportation purposes and a pair of electric storage heaters were fitted.

Their low power meant that the 1938 ballast motors were rarely used in pairs together, except for moving light loads such as a damaged car or two to Acton Works for repair. They were more often to be seen at one end of a ballast train which had a battery locomotive at the other end. Sometimes they were used in unusual combinations, such as the weed-killing pair (L150 and L151) which were coupled to the other end of the rail cleaning vehicle (F311) and a brake van from Metropolitan electric locomotive No.12, Sarah Siddons, for the 1979 leaf clearing season. At the time, the weed-killing cars were only being used as pilot motors. However, their original, dry pellet weed-killing system was used from time to time and it was eventually replaced by a new system which was fitted by Chipman's of Horsham. The cars went to Horsham late in 1985 and were returned on 22nd April 1986.

Two 1938 cars (10130-11130) were converted at Acton in March 1974 to form a 2-car yard electric locomotive. They were very similar in appearance to a conventional ballast loco conversion but they retained their five marker lights and did not get the flashing lamp bracket. They were additionally fitted with through power 'busline' cables so that the shoes of both cars were connected and could bridge long gaps in the conductor rails. The usefulness of this arrangement had first become apparent with the experimental articulated cars of 1935 stock which had worked as a 2-car shunter (L14A/B) at Acton until replaced by the 1938 unit. The latter was numbered L13A and L13B in the service stock list but retained its red livery until painted maroon in May 1978. It was withdrawn in May 1986 as it had become superfluous following the withdrawal of overhauls from Acton to the depots.

Two-car electric locomotive L13A/B, converted in 1974 from 1938 stock DMs 10130 and 11130. Brian Hardy

Another unusual conversion of 1938 stock was the pair of motor cars used to provide motive power for the Tunnel Cleaning Train. First authorised in 1971, this project eventually evolved into a 5-car train which was constructed at Acton Works between 1974 and 1978 when it emerged for a test run on 15th February. The two motor cars were numbered TCC1 (ex 10226) and TCC5 (ex 10087); the three intermediate vehicles were specially built by Acton and contractors. The design and construction of the train was very complicated and testing and modifications continued for some time afterwards. It saw little service over the next two years but began working more regularly during 1981. Its complexity has always proved a handicap, although when working it has performed well. In 1989 plans were being drawn up for its replacement.

Although ballast motor cars were used for taking staff to engineering worksites, it was always necessary to have some personnel carriers specifically for use with battery loco powered trains. Because of a shortage of personnel carriers during the late 1970s, 1938 ballast motors were sometimes included in a works train to act as the personnel carrier. In 1978, two 1938 NDMs were put aside for conversion to PCs but since they required the provision of handbrakes, which NDMs did not have, it was decided to convert motor cars instead. Three cars were converted, 11247 to PC857 in November 1980, 11165 to PC858 in December 1980 and 10165 to PC859 in February 1981.

An abortive conversion was carried out on trailer 012331 in 1978. In March 1978 it was converted for use as a track recording car. It was intended to replace two Standard stock trailers which had been part of a 4-car unit consisting of these trailers between two 1960 Cravens-built motor cars Nos.3910 and 3911. This unit had been used for track recording since 1971. The two motor cars were part of a batch of six 1960 tube stock cars which were hastily withdrawn when it was realised that they had been built with some internal linings made of a dangerous type of asbestos. The work of decontaminating four of these vehicles was carried out at White City, but 3910 and 3911 were not included, presumably because of the expense. As a result, the converted 1938 trailer, by now renumbered TRC912 and finished in service stock maroon with a white roof, remained in store at Acton until 1987 when it was transferred to Ealing Common for use as a stores vehicle.

Originally, a total of six 1938 trailers were earmarked for conversion to run with the 1960 stock motors. They were Nos. 012177, 012229, 012331, 012392, 012406 and 012408. Each was to have replaced two Standard stock trailers. The first to be done was 012392 which was completed in February 1976 and was formed into a 3-car unit with motors 3908/9 as No.4929. A second car, 4929 (ex-012229), was completed in April 1977 and was inserted between 3906/7. However, both units were soon withdrawn because of the asbestos scare and the trailers were stored. Trailer 012366 (not one of the originally chosen six) became 4921 in April 1978 and this was also put into store at Acton. In January 1980, 4929 became part of the 3-car test unit with motors 3902/3 for trials under the Full

Automatic Control of Trains (FACT) scheme. The other two re-entered service in December 1980 and March 1981 following the decontamination of the motor cars.

During their conversion, the 1938 trailers were fitted with fluorescent lighting, public address and a blue interior finish. Externally they were painted white to match the silver finish of their motor cars and had black roofs. They were also fitted with two compressors, de-icing equipment, sleet brushes and door fault indicator lights.

Another trailer, 012193, was sent to Metro-Cammell in Birmingham in 1974 in connection with some ventilation tests. Some of the windows were boarded up and square grilles were fitted to the ends and side of the car body. The car was returned to the Underground in 1976 and was scrapped in March 1980. The tests were used to demonstrate a pressure ventilation system which was eventually adopted for the 1986 tube stock and, incidentally, was built in to the track recording car TRC666.

Some withdrawn 1938 stock was used for training or testing. In 1971, a 3-car unit (10173) was permanently allocated to White City Depot for use by Rolling Stock Engineer's staff at the White City Railway Training Centre following the scrapping of the old 1920 stock training train in 1969. In February 1977, it was swapped for a complete 7-car train (10271-012279-11081+10299-012240-12043-11299) which had been withdrawn from the Northern Line. The 4-car unit from this train was replaced by unit 10280 in April 1978 so that it could form a 3-car unit (minus 12043) which became the last to get an EHO. Another 3-car unit (10306-012498-11247) was used as a pilot for the Experimental Tube Trains (ETT), since they were not permitted to operate under power over passenger lines except under an engineer's possession. Car 10306 was the 'sunshine window' car and last ran in service, with its 1949 stock trailer 012498, on 31st January 1978, just prior to its new duties as a pilot. Some rumours suggested that the car was to be saved for preservation but no-one started a fund for it and it was cut up at Ruislip in March 1980. Perhaps it was a classic case of everyone thinking someone else was doing something with the result that nobody did anything.

Some special sand drag tests were carried out at Upminster Depot in 1978 which involved the use of 1938 tube and CO/CP surface stock. The tests were conducted to find ways of protecting trains from the effects of high speed dead-end collisions like that at Moorgate in February 1975. The philosophy was based on the idea of reducing the speed of an approaching train to less than 20 mph and then providing some sort of collapsible barrier to absorb an impact at this speed. The speed reduction was achieved by the use of timed trainstop lowering as the train approached. The trials at Upminster were to test for collapsible barriers. The 1938 stock used consisted of 4 x 4-car units. The first units were sent to Upminster in March 1978 and tests were carried out there from time to time over the next few weeks. During the tests, the trains were rigged up so that they could be tested without a driver on board. The result of the tests was a large barrier of the type

Above The Underground's Tunnel Cleaning Train comprised a heavily-modified 1938 stock motor car at each end, and three purpose-built vehicles in between. When new, the train is seen in Ealing Common depot next to District Line CO/CP stock. Brian Hardy

Left In 1980-81, three Personnel Carriers were converted from 1938 stock motors to supplement those converted from Pre-1938 stock trailers in 1965-66. PC858 is seen in Neasden depot permanent way sidings. Brian Hardy

Below Originally intended to have been a Track Recording Car with 1960 Tube Stock Cravens-built motors, TRC912 (ex-012331), seen at Acton Works when newly converted in 1978, later moved to Ealing Common depot for use as a stores vehicle. Brian Hardy

Above **It was planned to replace pairs of Pre-1938 trailers in the 1960 stock by single 1938 trailers, but prohibitive costs meant that only three were done. Converted trailer 4929 is seen at Hainault, having been repainted in off-white and fitted with outside door indicator lights and de-icing equipment.** Brian Hardy

Left **Interior of a 1938 stock trailer converted for use with 1960 stock motor cars on the Hainault-Woodford branch. Fluorescent lighting and public address equipment has been fitted.** Brian Hardy

Below **Modified driving motor car 10306, which worked on the Bakerloo Line for a short time, spent most of its life on the Northern Line. Originally being at the outer end of a four-car unit, its latter days were spent at the inner end of a three-car unit, as seen here at Golders Green depot.** Brian Hardy

now seen at Ealing Broadway (Central) where a large pile of ballast is stacked behind a movable buffer. If the buffer is struck by a train, it is pushed into the ballast which absorbs the energy. Following the tests, the units were sent back to Neasden, the last eight cars going back in June.

Apart from the cars converted for test purposes, a further eight cars were given an unscheduled EHO and used to replace cars in damaged units which had already received an EHO. All were done while the main EHO programme was still under way. Three of the eight were in one complete 3-car unit (10213) which was given an EHO in 1976 to replace unit 10149. The cab of the motor car in the unit, 11149, survived to be used as a demonstration cab for the LT museum. It was later joined by 11182 which was preserved as a complete car and exhibited finished in 1950s condition. Two cars, 11036 and 12007, were scrapped as a result of a spectacular collision at Neasden on the morning of 7th July 1976. In this collision, a driver and a guard were killed and 25 cars of 1938 stock were involved as a result of a 7-car train hitting another 7-car train which, in turn, cannoned into a further 11 stabled cars. Car 11036 was replaced by 11055 (renumbered 11036) and 12007 by 12098.

Bakerloo and Jubilee

The long-awaited opening of the Jubilee Line finally took place when HRH Prince Charles conducted the official opening ceremony on 30th April 1979. Passenger service began on 1st May. Henceforth, in theory at least, the operation of the Bakerloo Line was to be restricted to the Elephant to Stonebridge Park section and the Stanmore branch became part of the Jubilee Line. In fact, there were occasional diversions from time to time and services were later extended north of Stonebridge Park to Harrow and Wealdstone.

As soon as the signalling on the new section of the Jubilee Line was available in the middle of August 1978, trial running began between Baker Street and Charing Cross. Crew training started almost immediately and 1938 stock was used indiscriminately with 1972 MkII stock. They were also to appear occasionally at times of crisis for a few weeks after the opening when Bakerloo trains were diverted to the Jubilee during service disruptions, although without passengers.

A new depot was built at Stonebridge Park for the maintenance of Bakerloo stock. Occasional trips for crew familiarisation were made from December 1977 but it was not until March 1978 that a large number of 1938 stock was transferred there for storage pending the opening of the Jubilee. During that March 5 x 7-car trains were transferred from Neasden to Stonebridge Park and a further three followed in April. On the day before the two lines were split, a carefully prepared stock utilisation plan was worked out to ensure that, at the end of the day, all the 1972 stock would finish at Jubilee Line stabling points and all the 1938 stock would finish at Bakerloo stabling points. As a result, the last 1938 at Stanmore left at 23.55 for Elephant.

Part of the equipment of the Bakerloo and Jubilee Lines involved 'Storno' radio. On the Bakerloo, ten driving cabs of 1938 stock trains were fitted with the equipment as part of the trial. Following many months of tests and in-service use it was eventually considered to be worth installing on all trains. The end cabs of all EHO trains were fitted with radio by early in 1979. In addition, following some trials with a new type of brake block with a low silica content supplied by Trist Draper, it was decided to equip all 1938 stock with the new blocks. As the change also involved increasing the air pressures of the braking systems, modified and unmodified units had to be kept separate for a time.

An EHO train of 1938 stock at the terminus of the Stanmore branch of the Bakerloo Line.
Capital Transport

Passing 1972 MkII stock in the southbound Bakerloo platform at Wembley Park, a 1938 stock train returns to Neasden depot via the northbound track in May 1979 shortly before transfer of the Stanmore branch to the Jubilee Line. Capital Transport

Just before the opening of the Jubilee Line, the Bakerloo saw another 'last' when the last unit expected to run in the old train red livery with gold transfers ran on 12th February 1979. Once the Bakerloo became separated from the Jubilee in May, little changed for the 1938 stock until November 1981 when two trains were withdrawn following service cuts introduced on 2nd November. One of the trains (10205-012292-11205 + 10297-012378-12048-11297) was transferred to White City to replace the training train which was scrapped. This left a total of 34 trains available to work a 24-train service. By now, the unreliability of the stock was causing problems and the reduction from 27 to 24 service trains was not equalled by the reduction in stock holding, which only involved two trains. One had been kept back to cover for the increased failures.

Following the decision in June 1980 to abandon any further construction of the Jubilee Line, the plans for withdrawal of all remaining 1938 stock were changed. It had been proposed to replace it with 1972 MkII stock displaced from the Jubilee Line when that line's new stock was introduced with the opening of its extensions. However, with the loss of these extensions, the only new stock required was for the replacement of the remaining 1938 stock. It was estimated that 28 trains, to be called 1983 stock, would be sufficient to equip the Jubilee Line. The 1972 stock on the Jubilee would be transferred to the Northern and 1959 stock from the Northern would go to the Bakerloo to replace the 1938 stock. This plan was modified following the Law Lords declaration of the illegality of the GLC fares subsidy policy. The legal decision required a doubling of fares which soon caused reductions in traffic. These were quickly followed by reductions in services. New timetables were introduced on all lines on 2nd December 1982. The tube lines now had a surplus of stock and it was quickly decided to reduce the order for 1983 tube stock to 15 trains. However, the replacement plan was unaltered as far as the Bakerloo was concerned – it was to have 31 trains of 1959 stock and all the 1938 stock would go. In the meantime, pending the delivery of the 1983 stock, the surplus 1959 stock thrown up by the service cuts was used to start the process of getting rid of the 1938 stock.

During the latter half of 1982, once this plan was known, withdrawals of 1938 stock began again and four trains had gone by the end of the year. Just the week after the start of the new timetable on 2nd December, the first 1959 stock arrived on the Bakerloo for crew training at Stonebridge Park and the first entered service on 28th February 1983. By October 1983, the Bakerloo had acquired the full surplus of 15 trains of 1959 stock and there were just 16 trains of 1938 stock left. In the meantime, the first of the 1983 stock had been delivered. It arrived in August 1983 but it was to be 1st May 1984 before it entered service.

North of Queen's Park there is a four-track shed, used for stabling trains overnight. During the day, however, the two centre tracks are used for reversing trains terminating at Queen's Park as seen here, while the two outside lines are for trains to/from Stonebridge and Harrow. As only London Underground trains use the fourth (negative) current rail north of Queen's Park, it was often policy to suspend the LUL service north of Queen's Park during adverse weather, as confirmed by the snow on the rails of No.21 road! Brian Hardy

The wholesale scrapping of the 1938/49 Tube Stock commenced in 1972 and much of the stock went by rail to various scrap dealers. On this occasion, this formation is passing through Handborough, north of Oxford, on 25th May 1978. Brian Hardy

At Bird's scrapyard in June 1978 there were over 40 cars of 1938 Tube Stock awaiting scrapping, of which a number are seen here. Brian Hardy

Some of the withdrawn 1938 Tube Stock was used for Sand Drag tests at Upminster, as a result of the Moorgate collision in February 1975. After the tests, the cars involved were only fit for travel by road to the scrapyard. Three pieces are seen at Neasden on 18th October 1978 to be taken away by Cashmores. Brian Hardy

One car of 1938 Tube Stock is now preserved in the London Transport Museum at Covent Garden. Driving motor car 11182 was restored to early-1950s condition and was taken by road from Ruislip to its new home on 15th September 1979. Brian Hardy

In 1973, three UNDM cars of 1938/49 Tube Stock were sold to the Army at MODAD, Bramley. Two cars later made their way to the Bicester Military Railway and are seen in their Army green en route in sidings west of Reading. Brian Hardy

In November 1984, a 7-car train of 1938 stock was restored to near original condition as part of a sponsorship deal with a West End theatre agency. It became known as the 'Starlight Express' and is seen here at North Wembley shortly after its overhaul.
Brian Hardy

In August 1984 there were sufficient 1983 stock trains available for service to allow the transfer of 1972 MkII stock to the Northern. The Northern then released more 1959 stock for the Bakerloo and withdrawals of 1938 stock started again, but slowly. Only three trains were withdrawn in 1984, the remaining 12 in 1985. The last train ran on 20th November 1985 formed thus:

10291-012371-11291+10012-012256-12027-11012

It ran only during the peak hours on its last day, the final trip being 18.52 Elephant to Stonebridge Park.

The train was the one known as the 'Starlight Express' which had been specially restored, largely as a result of the sponsorship of a West End theatre ticket agency. The agency had taken all of the advertising space on the train and each car advertised a West End show. One of the cars had advertising devoted to the musical 'Starlight Express', hence the nickname. The train was chosen because it contained car 10012, which had been in the first train to enter service in June 1938. Its original partner 11012 had been damaged in a collision at London Road in 1983 and was replaced by 11178 renumbered 11012. The train was restored at Stonebridge Park depot to near original condition. The exterior was finished in the traditional train red colour which had been standard on the Underground until the early 1970s and the window pillars were painted in cream as was done from new up to the 1950s. The roof was finished in the grey which the cars had when first delivered. The brown colour they had latterly was first applied during the war and involved the use of a very thick paint specially applied in order to overcome the problems of leaking roofs which the stock suffered in its early days.

Inside, the shovel type lampshades were restored and the cars were repainted as far as possible. The moquette seating had to remain as it was and the plastic armrests were retained but the original design of no-smoking labels was added. These labels read NON-SMOKING from the outside and NO-SMOKING from the inside. Old style route maps and interior transfers were specially produced for the restoration. The gilt transfers for the car numbers were included and LONDON TRANSPORT was applied to every car, as it had been done on all stock. It had been omitted from trailers and NDMs following an instruction issued in December 1953.

The train was completed in November 1984 and was given a special press run on 22nd of that month. It went back into normal passenger service shortly afterwards. Following its withdrawal after its last trip a year later, it was removed to Ruislip Depot on 5th December 1985 pending its possible use for tours.

The intended last day of operation of 1938 stock was 20th November 1985 and the 'Starlight Special' was used to perform the last trips on that day. R.J. Greenaway

Chapter 9
The Phoenix

The struggle to return to some sort of sanity in the fare structure following the 'Fares Fair' debacle and legal debates of 1982 led to a restructuring of the fare system in May 1983. This included a return to pre-1982 fare levels in real terms and the introduction of the Travelcard. Traffic levels then began to recover from their mid-1982 low and a 20% increase in tourist traffic in 1984 helped the recovery even further. The recovery rapidly turned into a sharp increase following the introduction of the Capitalcard in January 1985 and the improvement in the economy generally. It soon became apparent that services would have to be increased. Some trains were reinstated in 1986 but to provide for the traffic would require more rolling stock and, eventually, it was announced in September 1986 that 16½ additional trains of 1983 stock would be built.

At the same time, the organisation was under severe pressure from the Government to improve efficiency. One-Person Operation was first introduced on the Hammersmith & City Line in March 1984 and soon spread to all the other surface lines. Its introduction on the tube lines involved rather more complex equipment and operating rules than was required on the surface lines but agreement on a system had been secured with the Ministry of Transport by late in 1984 and development work continued throughout 1985. The conversion of 1973 tube stock began in March 1986 and it was planned that 1972 MkII and 1983 stock should follow. The conversion on the Piccadilly Line could be carried out on the available stock without affecting the service but this was not the case with the 1972 stock. Additional stock was needed to cover for those units under conversion. The answer was found in the 1938 stock.

The plan was first conceived as early as July 1985. The scrap dealers Booths were asked if they would agree not to take the last few units pending a decision on their future. Booths actually had a lorry at Ruislip and were in the process of loading a ballast motor car onto it when they were told about stopping the scrapping programme. Long telephonic negotiations took place while the loaders at Ruislip waited. Eventually, Booths agreed and the car was unloaded and put back on the tracks. Its partner, L155, had already gone, and this was the reason why an odd ballast car was scrapped instead of a pair as usual.

The scheme to re-introduce 1938 stock was strongly opposed by the then Operating Manager, John Cope. However, he was due to retire and would be gone by the time the programme came to fruition. With almost everyone else convinced that it was the only course open, much of the preparation work was done in secret. He retired in July 1986 and the scheme for rehabilitation was announced in August.

Early in August, the 7-car training train at White City (10205+10297) was sent to Ruislip with a view to protecting it and four other trains still there including the 'Starlight Express', from too much damage in case they could be used in service again. In April 1986, the idea of reinstating them had sufficient credibility for investigations to determine the cost of refurbishing them for further use. Soon after, the go-ahead was given for four trains to be prepared for service and the fifth kept as a spare. This was rightly seen as risky since the spare could be needed for service and so all five trains were given the treatment.

The first train to be dealt with was the 'Starlight Express', being the one needing least attention. It was completed in September 1986 and was sent to the Northern Line where it entered service on Monday 15th September. It attracted quite a lot of publicity at the time and featured in the press and on TV on a number of occasions over the next few weeks. The last of the five trains entered service on the Northern on 19th January 1987.

The refurbishment work was undertaken at Ruislip. It was largely the same sort of job normally done during an overhaul at Acton Works. It included lifting the cars and changing motors and equipment which had been overhauled at Acton, using a pool of equipment available from the scrapping programme. The trains were also fitted with Positive Train Identification equipment – as is standard on the Northern Line.

Bodywork repairs were needed around the windows where the vulnerable wooden finishing, always a source of trouble, had shown signs of rotting. Some panels had to be replaced and many cab floors needed replacement. The interiors were repainted in the traditional cerulean blue (which always looks green) and off-white (officially called Portland Stone), whilst exteriors were repainted to match the train red body with cream window pillars, gold LT transfers and grey roof of the 'Starlight Express'.

What was then thought to be the last 1938 Tube Stock train on the Northern Line ran on 14th April 1978, and was followed by a Farewell Tour on Sunday 4th June, using a seven-car EHO train borrowed from the Bakerloo Line. The train is seen at Edgware at the start of the tour. Brian Hardy

The first trains were done much more cheaply than originally expected. New parts were available from sub-stores, under workbenches etc, and many did not have to be booked out of stores where they would have been costed. A lot of 1938 stock parts had been written off from stores stock but not yet removed. They were thus effectively free and assisted in keeping the whole programme within the £450,000 budget.

It was originally expected that the last of the five trains would last until August 1988. This would have allowed them to have been in service for their 50th anniversary on June 30th. However, they proved troublesome in service, they retained the dislike of the crews and, regardless of the nostalgia market, the last (the 'Starlight Express' again) was withdrawn from service on 19th May 1988, just six weeks before its 50th birthday. On that day it worked in both peaks with its last scheduled trip from Edgware to Golders Green as train 112, 18.06½ to Morden arriving at 19.12. On this last trip, it lost 37 minutes due to pilot light problems between Hendon and Camden Town. However, it survived its last trip to Morden and the following day it was transferred to Ruislip.

Tours

The demise of the 1938 stock was accompanied by a coincidental gradual improvement in the attitude of LT towards the idea of running enthusiasts' specials. There had already been a softening of attitudes over the previous few years and, by 1973, after several earlier special train tours, it was realised that the organisation of special events was by no means impossible, given the necessary co-operation between departments and the dedicated help by interested members of staff at all levels.

The first tour using 1938 stock took place on Sunday 13th May 1973 using a 7-car train comprising:

10093-70525-31030+10054-012212-12088-11054

It began at Moorgate (Metropolitan) at 10.00 and worked over the Circle, East London and Metropolitan Lines to Amersham and Watford. It was such a success that a second tour was arranged for 14th October. This used a 6-car train from the Bakerloo:

10324-012497-11324+10097-012471-11097

The tour started from High Street Kensington and

The urgent need for more rolling stock on the Underground because of increased numbers of passengers meant that the five remaining trains of withdrawn 1938 Tube Stock in Ruislip depot were returned to service on the Northern Line, after an absence of over eight years. All five trains were overhauled at Ruislip depot and four were repainted into original livery to match the 'Starlight Express', which was the first to re-enter service on 15th September 1986. In the summer of 1987, a seven-car train is seen at Golders Green. Brian Hardy

Following the painting of units 10291 and 11012 into original livery, 1938 stock 'Starlight Express' railtours operated on Sundays 12th and 19th May 1985. These tours included the section of LMR line between Queen's Park and Kilburn High Road, where the fourth rail has been retained for emergency purposes. The train is seen in the 'up dc' platform at Kilburn High Road, before reversing beyond the station onto the down line. Brian Hardy

went to Olympia, Edgware Road, Hammersmith (Met), hence the need to keep the train length down to six cars, and then on to Wimbledon, Richmond, Golders Green, Arnos Grove and back to High Street Kensington. Bakerloo stock was used because it has special insulating shields fitted to the ends of the shoebeams to minimise earthing problems on sections of line where the BR third-rail current collection system is combined with the LT four-rail system. The Bakerloo encounters this situation north of Queens Park and it appears on the District Line branches to Wimbledon and Richmond.

A tour using eight cars was run on 2nd May 1976 covering the Metropolitan, District and Piccadilly Lines. This tour was notable in that the train visited New Cross and Lillie Bridge Depots. The next tour was arranged to commemorate the last of the 1938 stock on the Northern Line. It was run on Sunday 4th June 1978 with a 7-car train borrowed from the Bakerloo:

10205-012292-11205+10186-012270-12028-11186

The tour started from Golders Green then ran to

Edgware, Morden (including the depot) via Bank, High Barnet (via Bank), Park Junction, Mill Hill East, Kennington (Via Embankment), Golders Green, Euston (City), King's Cross (Piccadilly) then Cockfosters and finally finishing at Finsbury Park. The train was then sent on to Rayners Lane where it reversed to get back to Neasden for Bakerloo service on the Monday morning.

The next tours involving 1938 stock were the two which took place on two successive Sundays, 12th and 19th May 1985, using the 'Starlight Express'. The tour covered most of the Bakerloo, Jubilee, Metropolitan, District and Piccadilly Lines. It included trips into various places not normally seen by the passenger, including Stonebridge Park and London Road Depots, West Hampstead siding, Barking sidings, Acton Town east sidings and Upminster Depot. Heathrow Central was also visited by 1938 stock for the first time.

Following the stock's first withdrawal from service in 1985, the 'Starlight Express' was used for two identical tours on successive Sundays 30th March and 6th April 1986. Although it was officially advertised as 'The Farewell Tour', it was already a possibility that it would only be a temporary farewell. The itinerary included a start from White City, a trip over the connection between Ruislip Depot and the Metropolitan Line, Elephant, Harrow and Wealdstone, Elephant, Stanmore, Neasden Depot, Uxbridge, Acton Town, the Terminal 4 loop, which did not open to the public until 12th April and which was a first for 1938 stock, and then back to White City via Ealing Broadway.

Later on each day, the tour train reversed at Rayners Lane in the westbound platform. It is seen departing back onto the Metropolitan Line, having arrived from the Piccadilly Line, which included a trip around the Heathrow loop. Brian Hardy

The Isle of Wight

When the question of the replacement of the steam locomotives on the Isle of Wight was being discussed in the early 1960s, one of the least favoured options was electrification. However, it eventually became clear that it did have possibilities and, with the realisation that the very restricted loading gauge on the island might be accommodated by the use of redundant tube rolling stock from London, a plan began to emerge. It culminated with the introduction of electric services in March 1967 between Ryde and Shanklin using Standard tube rolling stock converted for the Southern Region 750 volt DC third rail traction system.

The stock used on the island was Standard tube stock which was being displaced from the Northern City Line by 1938 tube stock at that time. It was composed of a variety of types built between 1923 and 1934, so it was already between 33 and 44 years old when it arrived on the island. It was envisaged that it would last for about ten years, by which time there should be more tube stock available to replace it. As early as 1972, when the first bulk scrapping of the 1938 stock was being planned, it was suggested that 1938 stock would make an ideal replacement.

The story is told that, when BR approached LT in 1972 with a view to taking some 1938 stock, a senior engineer from the Underground told them that the stock was in such a bad condition that it was not worth the cost of repairing them. Whether the story is true or not, none were taken at the time and the Underground continued to use the stock for another 17 years. It was not until the very end of the life of the stock on the Underground that the idea was seriously raised again.

Discussions seem to have started during the final days of 1938 stock on the Northern Line early in 1988. At that time, it was considered that the ultimate goal would be the introduction of 1959 tube stock on the island. The 1938 stock would suffice for a few years until some of the aluminium bodied stock became available following its displacement by the new Central Line stock in the early 1990s.

Two formations of 1938 stock were suggested for the island. One was to have 2-car (M-M) units, the other was a 3-car (M-T-M) unit. The 3-car formation would have required the extension of the shed at Ryde to accommodate the extra train length. It was already going to be necessary to alter the track inside the shed to allow maintenance staff access to the sides of the underfloor equipment cases. The additional expense of lengthening the building was not considered worthwhile, so the 2-car formation was adopted.

BR agreed to take 34 cars from which to form eight 2-car units. The cars were completely rewired and a converter was provided to supply flourescent lights to replace the tungsten lighting. Since driving motor cars did not carry the air compressors when the stock worked on the Underground, the 11xxx car of each pair has had its motor generator removed and replaced by a compressor.

Only one guard's door control position is left on each unit, on the 10xxx car. Power buslines have been fitted between the cars of each unit to allow the removal of one set of shoegear at the trailing end of each car. The cars also had to be raised two inches on the bogies to allow clearance on the island. Whilst being worked over the mainland route they had to be temporarily raised a further inch. The budget for the whole job was originally £900,000.

The first seven cars for BR were moved from Ruislip depot to Strawberry Hill on 14th October 1988 and a further seven went on the 21st of the same month. A 4-car unit plus L148 went on 28th. It was planned that trains would be converted to 3rd rail current collection at Strawberry Hill and then sent to Eastleigh for overhaul and repainting in Network SouthEast livery. However, on 11th November a train was sent direct from Ruislip to Eastleigh. The last train of the batch, which included L149, went to Strawberry Hill on the 18th.

It was originally suggested that the first cars would be ready for the introduction of the Summer timetable in May 1989 but the work involved in rehabilitating the stock was considerable and the first unit was not ready until the beginning of July 1989. As at 1st July 1989, there were eight motor car pairs at Eastleigh Works, with one pair at Strawberry Hill (10229+11229) outstanding to be transferred. This last pair in fact made a test run on 12th June formed between two two-car SR EMUs from Strawberry Hill to Fratton via Teddington, Woking and Guildford, returning by the same route the following day. This was to 'gauge' the section between Haslemere and Fratton prior to driver training starting.

New Cars From Old

The refurbishment of the 1938 stock for the island has been very thorough. The outsides of the cars are finished in Network SouthEast livery. This extends up into the curve of the roof, almost to the top of door level. The grey and red colours sweep up diagonally at the driving ends and over the driving cab doors, over which rainstrips have been fitted. In addition to the NSE fleet name (at one end of the car) and car number (opposite end), the 'Island Line' name and logo is fixed to the side of the centre section, between the double door. The gutter at cant rail level has been covered over and the roof now fits flush with the top of the body. To prevent rain water running down and into the cars via the quarter light windows, the tops of the non-opening sections have been fitted with a rubber strip. The outside door indicator light on the roof has been moved downwards by about three inches to fit into the blue livery on the roof.

The inner (trailing) ends of the cars have been painted grey, rather than black as on most other NSE painted stock. At the driving ends, the surrounds to the cab windows are painted in black, while the rest below the cant line is in yellow. Above the cant rail line an area of light grey goes across the top, which is broken by the wing-shaped ventilator grilles, picked out in black. The bottom two headlights have been retained, while that in the centre is now a powerful spotlight. The two above have been blanked out. This arrangement is different from that shown on early publicity pictures and on 'The New Island Line Trains are Here' posters, where head and tail lights are shown as being in sealed twin units. A further difference in livery is that the yellow on the cab front goes down to the bottom of the body and does not stop short to have a thin white line across the bottom. The destination plate area (on the offside below the cab window) and the train set number position in the front cab door, have been retained. The unit number is shown under the driver's cab window, but not the class number.

The new interior finish of the stock is blue, grey and cream/white. Flourescent lighting fed by an inverter has been fitted – two 40W tubes on each side of the car per seating bay. There is also a shaded section of flourescent lighting above each doorway position. The woodwork around the windows and at the car saloon ends has been replaced by totally new varnished beechwood. New, grey, speckled linoleum has been fitted to the car floors, but at the doorway positions there is a ridged rubber finish. New stainless steel seat risers are fitted. The seating is just as comfortable as when with London Underground, but the moquette used is Network Blue Blade. Longitudinal seating positions are separated by standard armrests painted in blue. The interior ceilings have been replaced by aluminium, sprayed off-white. The door interiors are finished in Network (dark) grey, while other paintwork is in light (smoke) grey. For the standing passenger, the ceiling mounted handholds have been removed and replaced by grab rails, except over the doorway areas, where there are none. Unlike the Pre-1938 tube stock, no luggage 'pens' have been provided and the basic layout of the cars is unchanged.

As mentioned above, all the equipment on the 1938 tube stock is being overhauled and the trains completely rewired. A compressor is fitted on the 'D' cars, while the guard will operate from the 'A' cars. The guard's panel appears very much as it was with London Underground, but additional communications equipment has been provided – cab to cab, guard to driver and public address to passengers. There is not, at present, any restriction on passengers using the end single doors of these trains (except when occupied by the guard, of course). Passenger door control has been (re)fitted, activated by the guard pressing a 'P' (passenger) open button. As on other modern SR sliding door stock, it is also possible for passengers to close the doors. On the car exteriors, the buttons are mounted in the original positions, but on the inside the open buttons stand proud of the original position. Heating is provided in the traditional underseat positions, supplemented by fan heaters at doorway positions.

Miniature circuit breakers have replaced fuses in the cabs and new speedometers have been provided. The driver has a fan heater by the cab seat. New window wipers have been fitted, and a chime whistle is fitted next to the top of the driver's cab window on the nearside.

1938 Stock on the Island
The first two-car unit to be completed made its first trip outside Eastleigh Works on Friday 30th June 1989 (exactly 51 years to the date that the stock first entered passenger service). It made one round test trip to Winchester on that day and on Monday 3rd July, before being transferred, under its own power, from Eastleigh to Fratton on Tuesday 4th July. From there it was shipped to the island on the 01.00 ferry from Portsmouth to Fishbourne.

The cars remained at Fishbourne overnight and were taken by road to Sandown for railing on the Wednesday morning. They were formed up there as unit 483.001 and were towed to Ryde at 04.50 the next morning using a Standard stock four-car unit plus one more motor car. At 18.30 that evening, after the 20-minute service had been 'thinned out', the unit was eased out into the depot sidings and, after shunting back into the down platform road, a crew training run was operated to Shanklin. The 1938 tube stock had begun yet another new lease of life.

The official ceremony to inaugurate 'The Island Lines New Train Fleet' was held on Thursday morning 13th July 1989. Invited guests made their way to Ryde Pier Head, while the two-car unit of 1938 Tube Stock left the depot at 10.18 and worked empty to Ryde Esplanade. It then worked to the south end of Pier Head station, while Mr Chris Green, Director of Network SouthEast, made a speech. He said that NSE were totally committed to the Island Line with the 'new' trains and with the modernisation of the stations. He also hinted that improvements were needed for the permanent way on the Island, which has a shingle base, as the 1938 stock gave a lively ride on it whereas on the mainland the ride was much more solid.

At the 'launch', the two-car unit made its way into Pier Head station and broke a banner stretched across platforms 2 and 3. The guests were then able to inspect the train and then take a trip in it south to further ceremonies at Smallbrook Junction and Brading.

As the ceremony on Thursday 13th July marked the start of 'Gala Week' on the Isle of Wight, the 1938 unit worked the Pier shuttle service daily during the mid-day period until Wednesday 19th July (except for a rail strike day, the 18th). After, it was planned that the unit would not carry passengers for some weeks, so that testing could take place. A test was carried out on August 2nd and, on 23rd August, three round trips were made during the mid-morning period.

Units 002 and 003 arrived on the island on the 26th and 28th September respectively and a 6-car test run took place on October 2nd. The first official entry in service took place on Saturday 7th October 1989.

With its public introduction as the 'new' stock for the Isle of Wight fifty-one years after its introduction on the London Underground as a revolutionary new design, the 1938 Tube Stock has surely had a remarkable career in rail transport. From its early teething troubles, followed by a world war and a subsequent reorganisation of its form and use, it finally settled down to a fifteen-year period of steady and relatively uneventful service. It was then thrown into the financial and political turmoil of the early 1970s which marked the beginning of its end. This end, however, was a long time coming and, even then, came twice.

Above **Following its final withdrawal from passenger service on the Underground, some 1938 stock was sold to BR for use on the Isle of Wight. Stock was transferred from Ruislip Depot to Clapham Junction in the first stage of its journey to Eastleigh for refurbishment.**
R.J. Greenaway

Left **The first refurbished unit of 1938 stock arrived on the Isle of Wight on 5th July 1989. Here newly renumbered and repainted car 221 is about to be lifted onto its bogies at Sandown on the Island.**
R.J. Greenaway

Part of the publicity about the arrival of 1938 stock on the Isle of Wight, this banner was photographed at Ryde Esplanade in mid-July 1989.
R.J. Greenaway

The official launch of 1938 stock on the Isle of Wight occurred on 13th July 1989. At Ryde Pier Head, the official party is just about to board the train. The Director of Network SouthEast, Chris Green, accompanied by his wife, is on the right.
R.J. Greenaway

The interior of class 483, as 1938 stock is now officially known on Network SouthEast, has been completely rebuilt and finished in a pleasing mixture of blue, grey, off-white and natural wood. The cars also have fluorescent lighting, public address and passenger door controls.
R.J. Greenaway

The 1938 stock has been formed into 2-car units for the Isle of Wight and a very thorough and beautifully finished refurbishment job has been done by staff at Eastleigh. Here the first unit to be completed, No.001, is on show at Ryde. R.J. Greenaway

Appendix
1938 Stock Dimensions and Numbering

MAIN DIMENSIONS OF 1938 TUBE STOCK

	DM Car	NDM Trailer
Length over body	52ft 3¾ins	51ft 2¾ins
Bogie centres	33ft 6 ins	33ft 3 ins
Bogie centre to body rear	8ft 11⅞ins	8ft 11⅞ins
Bogie centre to body front	9ft 9⅞ins	8ft 11⅞ins
Bogie wheelbase	3ft 6 ins	3ft 6 ins
	+2ft 9 ins	+2ft 9 ins
Wheel diameter	2ft 7 ins	2ft 7 ins
Height above rail	9ft 5½ins	9ft 5½ins
Floor height	2ft 3 ins	2ft 3 ins
Floor to cant rail	5ft 0 ins	5ft 0 ins
Door height	6ft 2½ins	6ft 2½ins
Double doorway	5ft 1½ins	5ft 1½ins
Single doorway	2ft 6¾ins	2ft 6¾ins
Double door opening	4ft 6 ins	4ft 6 ins
Single door opening	2ft 3 ins	2ft 3 ins
Width over sills	8ft 10ins	8ft 10ins
Width over body	8ft 6¼ins	8ft 6¼ins
Seats	42	40

CAR WEIGHTS

Driving motor car	27.4 tons
Trailer	20.65 tons
Non-driving motor	25.9 tons
7-car train	176.9 tons empty, 250.9 tons loaded

SUMMARY OF 1938 TUBE STOCK NUMBERING

All cars built by Metro-Cammell except those marked 'Birmingham'

Type of car	Numbering
'A' driving motors	10012-10323
'D' driving motors	11012-11323
'A' driving motors (9-car trains)	90324-90333
'D' driving motors (9-car trains)	91324-91333
Non-driving motors	12000-12028
	12409-12411
	12422-12446
Non-driving motors (Birmingham)	12059-12157
Non-driving motors (9-car trains)	92029-92058
Special non-driving motors	92447-92466
Trailers (Birmingham)	012158-012388
	012412-012421
	012467-012476
Trailers (9-car trains – Birmingham)	092389-092408
Trailers (converted from 1935 motors)	012477-012497
Trailers (1949 Birmingham)	012498-012515
Trailers (Miscellaneous conversions)	012022,012151
	012516-012517
Trailers (1927 built, 1938 conversions)	70513-70570
'A' UNDMs (1949 Birmingham)	30022-30045
'D' UNDMs (1949 Birmingham)	31000-31045
'A' UNDMs (1949 conversion)	30000-30021

RENUMBERING BY SOUTHERN REGION

LUL Numbers	NSE Numbers	Unit Number	LUL Numbers	NSE Numbers	Unit Number
10184	121	483001	11184	221	483001
10221	122	483002	11221	222	483002
10116	123	483003	11116	223	483003
10205	124	483004	11205	224	483004
10142	125	483005	11142	225	483005
10297	126	483006	11297	226	483006
10291	127	483007	11291	227	483007
10255	128	483008	11255	228	483008
10229	129	483009	11229	229	483009

121-129 are 'A' end cars and 221-229 are 'D' end cars